FIVE
KILOS IN
5 WEEKS

This book is dedicated to you and your inspired self, for picking it up and having the willpower, determination and commitment to change your life for the better. I hope this book helps you to cultivate a positive mindset, move your body each day and cook delicious food that nourishes you inside and out.

LOSE WEIGHT SAFELY WITH A SIMPLE DIET PLAN THAT ACTUALLY WORKS!

FIVE KILOS IN 5 WEEKS

LUKE HINES

plum. Pan Macmillan Australia

FIVE IN FIVE

CONTENTS

WHAT IS THE 5 IN 5?

The 5 in 5 is designed to bring back your confidence so you can love the skin you're in.

The 5 in 5 is here to help you feel happier, healthier and more in tune with yourself.

The 5 in 5 is a holistic approach to living well without needless restriction and stress.

The 5 in 5 is a sustainable approach to losing the first, middle or last 5 kg.

The 5 in 5 creates a healthy relationship between you, food and eating well.

The 5 in 5 is suitable for adults of all ages and fitness levels.

The 5 in 5 sets you up with the tools you need for long-term wellbeing.

The 5 in 5 introduces you to real food that tastes great and is great for you.

The 5 in 5 is designed to work for you and your lifestyle.

The 5 in 5 is designed to bring out your best self.

The 5 in 5 is a chance to make YOU a priority.

The 5 in 5 features 60 easy real-food recipes with ONLY 5 core ingredients (or fewer).

The 5 in 5 is delicious.

The 5 in 5 is simple.

The 5 in 5 is fun.

The 5 in 5 works.

And the 5 in 5 starts now!

INTRODUCTION

I've been in the 'wellness' industry for 20 years now, and I'm excited to share with you everything I've learned and experienced to date, in this easy-to-follow plan that actually works.

Starting out as a group fitness instructor when I was 19 years old, I fell in love with how I felt when moving my body. Enjoying my time spent in the gym led me to become a one-to-one personal trainer, and in the following years I built a strong reputation training people from all walks of life, from big-name Hollywood celebrities to everyday humans like you and me, who just needed the right support and guidance to change their lives for the better.

Throughout the years, though, I realised that no matter how hard I trained my clients during our sessions, it was what happened outside those sessions that mattered so much more. How they slept, managed stress, moved incidentally and, most importantly, how they ate. The food they consumed made the difference between either regressing, stagnating or thriving. And that's when I prioritised where nutrition sits in the overall picture of living confidently in our own skin.

I returned to study and became a functional nutritionist so I could provide the most up-to-date, relevant and results-based advice to my clients, and the flow-on effect was that my cookbooks benefited from my knowledge. In each one the focus was on real food nutrition that reduced inflammation, naturally encouraged weight loss and lean muscle maintenance, and held the key to becoming energised, healthy and well.

Now, that's where this book comes into play. Despite having healthy recipes at our fingertips and the best of intentions to eat well, exercise and make positive lifestyle choices, sometimes we just don't. And, hey, there are lots of reasons why (and we will get into that shortly), but in life we sometimes need a gentle nudge, a little bit of support, or a massive kick in the butt, to remind us that no goal is impossible, too far gone or too late to achieve. And anyone, of any age, can make some simple changes that mean a long-term lifelong difference.

And let me just tell you, you're NOT alone. Despite knowing all the right things to do, I've also gone through periods where I've done the exact opposite of what I know I should be doing. In 2021 I gained 15 kg of excess body fat. The combination of COVID lockdowns and some work I needed to do on my own mental health was the perfect storm for what happened to me, physically and mentally. I lost my drive, motivation and inner spark. I became addicted to poor food choices, was tired all the time, and didn't feel comfortable in my own skin. I decided to share my weight-loss journey publicly to show that we're all human and even someone who knows what they're doing can struggle. The real highlight, though, was experiencing what so many people go through each day and then using my knowledge to get back to my authentic self, inside and out. I tracked my progress, kept a record of my method, and now, through that lived experience, plus my many years of experience as a trainer and healthy cook, I can provide you with a realistic and achievable way for you to do this too.

And that's how the 5 in 5 was born.

If anything so far has resonated with you, or you've ever felt trapped, stuck or weighed down by your current physical condition or mindset, and you want to make a change, this is the plan for you.

We're an interesting bunch, us human beings. We can have all the tools to make positive change at our disposal, but until they're laid out in an easy-to-follow, digestible way (haha, pun intended), we don't do anything about it. And that's exactly why I created the 5 in 5: to take the guesswork out of looking and feeling your best.

Not only will I guide you through the steps to lose 5 kg in 5 weeks in a safe, sustainable and delicious way, but I also provide you with more than 60 easy-to-follow recipes that contain only 5 core ingredients or fewer – meaning your meals will always be quick, simple, affordable *and* tasty. You'll learn more about the recipes and meal plans in the pages to come.

Also, you'll learn how to cook the BEST types of food to get long-term results without skimping on flavour.

You'll learn how to manage your portion sizes, quench any cravings and keep living a normal social life while still reaching your goals.

And, very importantly, you'll learn the habits and behaviours that supplement how you eat, to bring everything together – from how to move to ways to think more positively and tools to stay on track.

The best part is, you'll never feel like you're on a diet. Because the 5 in 5 is not about deprivation, starvation or limitation, it's about education, expansion and freedom.

One of my favourite things about life is that no matter how many decisions we make that don't support the lives we want to live, we are only one small decision away from course-correcting our path and stepping into our potential.

So, hold on tight! This book isn't just do what I say; it's do what I did and continue to do – I have been where you are, and I know what needs to be done. Now, c'mon, let's lose 5 kg in 5 weeks and have a delicious, inspiring and life-changing time doing it!

Luke xx

HOW AND WHY DO WE PUT ON WEIGHT?

Some people are really in tune with their bodies and minds and understand exactly why they've gained weight, lost track of their goals and aren't feeling or looking their best. Others wake up one day, take a look in the mirror and feel like overnight they've gone from being really confident about themselves to feeling self-conscious in their own skin, lacking motivation and being their own worst enemy. Regardless of where you sit on that spectrum, it's important to acknowledge and understand the core reasons we put on excess weight. And, for the purposes of this book, when I talk about excess weight, I'm referring to unwanted body fat, not lean muscle mass (but we will talk about that later).

1. Eating too much

Consuming more calories than we expend is the most basic of weight-gain principles. Whether the calories are from fat, protein or carbs, if we consume more energy than we utilise, the rest is stored in our bodies as excess body fat. It's important to remember that even consuming an excess of what is considered 'healthy food' can result in unintentional weight gain.

2. Not moving enough

Just as consuming more calories than our body requires leads to weight gain, lack of movement compounds this problem. Sedentary lifestyles and behaviours – such as sitting all day, excessive screen time and lack of incidental or structured exercise – are all contributing factors to storing and gaining body fat, regardless of how you eat.

3. Eating the wrong types of food

Beyond the basic energy-in versus energy-out equation, eating the wrong types of food can also trigger, encourage or promote weight gain. Processed and refined foods and foods that are high in sugar are linked directly to unintentional weight gain and the associated illnesses and/or disorders that come with consuming them, including type 2 diabetes, insulin resistance and cardiovascular disease.

4. Poor-quality or lack of sleep

The importance of sleep is up there, along with diet, exercise and mindset, when it comes to being truly well. In fact, I prioritise it with how I eat and how hard I train, as it links back to all aspects of our lives – including our weight. Not only does poor-quality or lack of sleep affect our cognitive function, physical performance and recovery, but studies have shown insufficient sleep is linked to an increase in body fat and a decrease in lean muscle mass.

5. Stress

Stress and the associated stress hormone cortisol are directly linked to weight gain. Not only does cortisol increase our hunger, but it is responsible for regulating our metabolism – and it, in fact, slows it down. Studies have shown high levels of cortisol in our body are linked to the craving and consumption of highly processed, refined, salty, sweet and fatty foods. Ever felt stressed out and reached for a block of chocolate or packet of chips? You now know why.

6. Hormonal or health condition

It would be remiss of me to summarise weight loss or gain as being as simple as energy in versus energy out when hormonal, inflammatory, autoimmune or chronic health conditions have a dramatic impact on how we hold on to and gain excess weight. Hormonal imbalances, such as polycystic ovary syndrome (PCOS), hypothyroidism, diabetes, insulin resistance and depression, can all contribute to unintentional weight gain.

WELL, WHAT CAN WE DO ABOUT IT?

The good news is, once we identify why we as individuals might be putting on weight, we can go about finding a suitable way to do something about it. And this book isn't just about how you look, it's about how you feel inside, which is then reflected on the outside. When you're thriving, with good digestion, absorbing your nutrients with great gut health, bursting with energy, waking up pain-free and feeling positive, naturally the by-product of that is glowing skin, bright eyes and a reduction in, and long-term solution to, excess weight gain. With the help of this plan, you'll have all the tools and techniques you need to successfully lose 5 kg in 5 weeks in a realistic and sustainable way.

1. Eat the right amount of food

Eating too much food leads to excess weight gain. In this book I will show you how to eat the right amount of food so you are never hungry, never feel like you're on a diet, and you are fuelled in a way that optimises mental, physical and emotional performance and energises your day. The recipes and structured meal plans will set you up to learn how much you need to eat for real results, plus you'll reduce cravings, eliminate binge-eating and thrive as your best self.

2. Move your body and actually enjoy it

If you're already eating fairly well, once we really home in on your individual calorie needs, we will look at how exercise supplements your nutrition, and how we can use it to maintain or even expedite your results. Moving your body is key to balancing the calorie intake equation, along with improving your mood, helping you sleep better and keeping you fit and well for life. And if you're interested in muscle gain, how you train and how you fuel that movement is pivotal to your growth success – more on that to come.

3. Eat the right types of food and make it taste great

You need to understand the best food to support the wellness you want in your life. At its core, the 5 in 5 is about reducing processed, refined and high-sugar foods; from there we need to dig deeper and look more closely at real wholefoods and how key macronutrients – proteins, fats and carbs – can work in your favour to get results. In the 5 in 5 eating plan I'll introduce you to recipes and ingredients that not only make a positive difference to your health, but taste great too.

4. Learn how to sleep better

The importance of sleep and its direct link to how we store and gain excess weight is a crucial factor to consider. This is a holistic plan that considers various lifestyle factors that are detrimental to our sleep, and provides tips and solutions on how you can manage them. The tools and techniques you'll learn will make this journey so much easier and a whole lot more enjoyable. Because, let's be honest, we all feel much better after a good night's sleep.

5. Reduce and manage stress

Stress is something that is inevitable in life, whether we like it or not. Now, rather than fearing the various stressors that we are faced with, if we acknowledge what they are and use a tool kit of techniques to manage them better, we're going to minimise or even eliminate the negative impact stress has on our bodies. Stress can affect how we perform and can contribute to weight gain. This plan takes stress and how you manage it seriously, so you get the results you want and feel better for it.

6. Get the help you need for any hormonal or health imbalance

When it comes to the various hormonal, inflammatory, autoimmune or chronic health conditions that affect weight gain, it's so important to acknowledge them and get the professional help you need to manage them. Some may be curable, others potentially placed into remission and some managed in a way that decreases the impact on your life. This is where the support, guidance and help of a professional makes such a difference. If you fall into the category of having a health or hormonal condition, don't be afraid to get support that can supplement what you do here with the 5 in 5. You're not alone with your struggles, and sometimes the first step to making a change is being brave enough to seek the help you need.

LET'S GET THIS STRAIGHT: THIS ISN'T A QUICK-FIX SOLUTION

The reason I have structured this program to be 5 in 5 is simple: it's a manageable, tangible amount of time that avoids the pitfalls of those quick-fix fad diets that promise rapid weight-loss results. When we lose too much weight too quickly, it can have a detrimental effect on our minds and bodies. Unsafe weight loss can affect our digestion, energy, mood and hormonal balance; not to mention, when done too quickly, we mostly lose fluid and vital muscle mass. By losing 5 kg in 5 weeks, you're setting yourself up for long-term success, without the risk of yo-yoing back to where you started, or worse, gaining even more weight. So please, trust the process and allow your intuitive body to adjust, adapt and transform – and let's do it from a place of love.

TO COUNT CALORIES OR NOT TO COUNT CALORIES?

Now, this may be controversial, but you'll notice the unit of measurement I use is calories, not kilojoules. I know the official Australian measurement is technically kilojoules, but with such a heavy influence from the USA and UK in Australian media and products, most people are very familiar with calories. I want this book to be approachable for the entire world, so I'm sticking with calories to make it easy and simple to understand for all. Plus, if I'm totally honest, it's my preferred unit of measurement by far. I find the smaller number is easier to manage mentally throughout my day.

If you're wondering what the difference is, 1 kilojoule = 0.24 calories, so just under a quarter. To convert the calories in these recipes to kilojoules, simply multiply the total calories by 4.18 and you're pretty much there.

Let's start with the basics first for those who are new to this world. A calorie is a form of measurement that describes both the energy our body gets from food, and the energy we need and use to perform life's basic functions, such as maintaining our heartbeat, thinking, even breathing. But beyond those primal needs, calories are what fuel our day, help us lift things, push things, carry things and do things.

We get calories from both food and drinks, and these calories are sourced from the key macronutrients (macros) of proteins, fats and carbs, with varying amounts of calories found in each:

CARBS: 4 calories per gram
FATS: 9 calories per gram
PROTEIN: 4 calories per gram

It's important to mention alcohol here. While it's not a macronutrient or a food group, alcohol contains 7 calories per gram, which is why on this program I strongly advise to avoid it. Trust me, I have been doing this long enough to know how you'll succeed. I am only asking for 5 weeks, so stick with me on that one, please. Not only is it high in empty calories (more on that shortly), but it's a depressant that will slow down your mental state and recovery and lower your mood.

So, if we consume more calories than we require in a day, is absolutely *everything* that is excess stored as fat? Not quite. Once our bodies' daily requirements are met, the excess calories, or shall we say, energy, is stored as either glycogen – in our muscles and liver – or fat. If we bring ourselves back to the equation of energy in versus energy out, when we eat too much, especially of the wrong types of food, we gain excess body weight in the form of body fat.

In order to achieve optimal results on this plan, I highly encourage counting calories, and have made that a key component here. Because for this short 5-week period, I want to be absolutely sure that you know exactly what your body needs to get the results you want, and sometimes that takes looking at things a little more closely. And that's why I've taken the guesswork out for you by calculating the calories for every single recipe and structuring the meal plans so you hit your daily targets and stay on track. All you need to do is follow the plan – it's as simple as that.

THE 5 IN 5
UP WITH T
YOU NEED
TERM WEL

SETS YOU
HE TOOLS
FOR LONG-
LBEING.

CALORIE INTAKE, A CLOSER LOOK

Now that you know we are going to be counting calories, let's take a look why. Put simply, you need to be in a calorie deficit state to lose weight, a calorie balanced state to maintain weight, and in a mindful calorie surplus to gain lean muscle mass safely without gaining too much body fat.

CALORIE DEFICIT (500–700 less calories per day)	CALORIE MAINTENANCE (TDEE – total daily energy expenditure)	CALORIE SURPLUS (Extra 300–500 calories per day)
When in a state of calorie deficit, you will lose body fat (or muscle mass if taken to the extreme with lack of food or over-exercising).	When in a calorie-balanced state, you will maintain your current weight and either remain in the same physical condition or recomposite your body by following correct training and nutrition protocols.	When in a state of calorie surplus, you will increase body fat (or muscle mass if done properly with training).

LET'S UNPACK EACH

Calorie deficit

Studies have proven that your body weight will respond according to your daily calorie intake. Having a safe daily calorie deficit will promote a decrease in body fat, and that's made a whole lot easier when following a diet balanced with quality proteins, unrefined carbs and good fats. Be mindful that in a calorie deficit state achieved by over-exercising, or not eating enough protein in particular, you will not only lose body fat but also crucial lean muscle mass, and considering how hard lean muscle mass is to gain, you want to avoid this for many health reasons.

Calorie maintenance

I often refer to this as the balance or maintenance phase, where the energy you're consuming matches the energy you're exerting. Without proper training it's likely you'll maintain your current body composition, but with correct exercise and strict nutrition, this maintenance phase can also be a good time for recompositing your physique, by increasing lean muscle mass and decreasing body fat, but it takes a long time and you've got to be strict. Be patient as it's a very slow and steady process. The calories required for this phase are often referred to as TDEE (total daily energy expenditure), which we'll learn more about shortly.

Calorie surplus

A calorie surplus from poor nutrition, excessive calorie consumption and inadequate movement is what we want to avoid, as it leads to unwanted excess weight gain. It's important to mention that those who want to increase lean muscle mass substantially and put size on, through the process of strength training, need to be in a mindful calorie surplus, around 300–500 extra calories per day than your TDEE. I say 'mindful' because it isn't a free-for-all. You can still gain body fat, but how much body fat you gain compared to muscle mass you develop will come down to the quality of food you eat, how hard you train (the correct stimulus on your muscles for growth) and the right lifestyle factors, such as quality sleep and stress management. Anything above a surplus of 500 calories per day will be a sure-fire way to excess body fat storage.

Because the 5 in 5 has a structured meal plan, measurable timeline and supporting lifestyle activities, I advise the counting and measuring of calories for accuracy of results. You don't have to do it forever, but tracking your calories for this period of time is a really good way to check in with where your daily food intake is now and shift what you've not been able to shift before. I've had clients experience incredible insights. Some, by measuring what they eat across a week, realise they are consuming way more calories than they need, which gives them an explanation as to why they're gaining and storing excess fat. Whereas others discover they're not eating enough, and other lifestyle factors are contributing to their weight, which gives them the knowledge to get the advice and support they need. Regardless, having the information provides us with somewhere to start. Knowledge is power.

My hope with this plan is for you to feel confident enough after the initial 5 weeks to decide whether you'd like to continue counting calories or not, and if this is sustainable for you moving forward. You might love the structure, accuracy and results that counting calories provides; alternatively, you may choose to stop counting them, and instead look to a more intuitive approach where you tune in and listen to your body. And this takes me to my next point.

You can absolutely still follow the 5 in 5 plan even if you aren't a fan of counting calories. For some, calorie counting can be triggering or can encourage an unhealthy relationship with food; for others it may be that they don't have the time or patience. And that's okay, that's where intuitive eating comes into play.

Intuitive eating

Intuitive eating is where you tune in and listen to your body, take note of how you feel and look, and make decisions based on your performance and the results you achieve each week. It's about having the willpower and self-awareness to eat when you're genuinely hungry, know when you've had enough and stop when you're full. If you're feeling tired, unable to exercise and are losing mental focus, perhaps this is when you need to increase your daily calories; whereas if you can't seem to shift any weight, find yourself snacking for no reason and keep reaching for the wrong types of food, this is when you might need to tighten things up and bring yourself back to the core 5 in 5 principles to ensure great results. Humans are clever, if we listen to our bodies and focus hard enough on how we are thinking, feeling and performing, we can usually work out what's going on and act accordingly; so check in with yourself and evolve, adapt and align.

A NOTE ON DISORDERED EATING

If you've ever felt or feel you could experience some form of disordered eating by counting calories, tracking workouts and generally focusing this closely on what you eat and how you move, don't count the calories or track your workouts; instead, be kind to yourself and follow a more intuitive eating approach as described above.

I understand that the level of commitment to accuracy I am asking for isn't for everyone, and that's okay. You need to be gentle with yourself and do what works for you. If you begin to experience feelings of stress, anxiety, shame or guilt around food and exercise, please don't put extra pressure on yourself. Simply do the 5 in 5 in a way that works for you, and if need be, seek the help of a health professional. You're not alone in any of this.

HOW MANY CALORIES A DAY SHOULD I EAT?

Before we look at how to calculate your accurate individual calorie needs, we need to first understand our basal metabolic rate (BMR) and total daily energy expenditure (TDEE).

Your BMR is the number of calories your body expends in a resting state for basic survival, performing critical functions for our brains, kidneys, lungs, digestive system, nervous system and heart. Then, on top of that we need to calculate the calories required for everything else, such as physical activity, exercise and recovery, and if we want to stay exactly the same, not lose or gain, this number is referred to as our TDEE.

The calories you need to consume per day vary depending on several factors including your age, sex, activity level, height and weight. Plus, keeping in mind the calories-in versus calories-out principle, you can exercise more and eat however much you want, or exercise less and watch what you eat a little more closely, as long as you're in a calorie deficit state.

What you won't get from me on this plan is anything drastic, unrealistic or unsustainable. Over the years in the fitness industry, I have seen books, online programs and influencers spruik dangerously low daily calorie recommendations – as low as 1000 calories per day. So, despite the fact you'll quickly lose water weight and vital lean muscle mass, you're setting yourself up for a massive potential rebound of rapid weight gain, potentially more than you started out with. Not only is this approach to weight loss unrealistic, but it can lead to serious health issues, such as metabolic conditions, digestive issues, nutrient deficiencies and an unhealthy relationship with food.

To understand how many calories you should be eating for weight loss, we need to look at what our TDEE calories need to be; that is, the number of calories we need to stay in maintenance phase – not lose and not gain, just to stay the same. Here are the current recommendations:

WOMEN

AGE	DAILY CALORIE REQUIREMENT FOR MAINTENANCE
18–30	2000–2400
31–60	1800–2200
61+	1600–2000

MEN

AGE	DAILY CALORIE REQUIREMENT FOR MAINTENANCE
18–30	2400–3000
31–60	2200–3000
61+	2000–2600

When looking at those numbers, you need to be aware that there is no one-size-fits-all approach. Because, along with sex, age, height, weight and activity level, we need to take into account metabolic health, cardiovascular health, physical demands and health conditions.

You'll notice I do not offer or discuss the calories required for children under 18. I am a big believer in building a healthy and strong relationship between kids and food that doesn't involve calorie counting, a focus on weight loss, or any mention of body image. In these pivotal years we have to be really mindful about how we talk about our bodies and what we value as important, and set young people up for making their own decisions when they are mature enough to do so.

Of course, it should be acknowledged that not everybody identifies as male or female. If you have any questions about your own calorie requirement or BMR numbers – or the total daily energy expenditure numbers opposite – and how they relate to you, please consult a healthcare professional.

CALCULATING YOUR TDEE

To understand what your individual calorie deficit is, we first need to calculate your total daily energy expenditure (TDEE).

STEP 1

Calculate your basal metabolic rate (BMR): the number of calories required to simply stay alive before any activity or movement. You'll need to know your current weight and height, along with your age.

WOMEN: BMR = 10 x weight (kg) + 6.25 x height (cm) – 5 x age (years) – 161

MEN: BMR = 10 x weight (kg) + 6.25 x height (cm) – 5 x age (years) + 5

So, take me for example, my BMR is 900 + 1193.75 – 195 + 5 = 1903.75 calories, just to function.

STEP 2

Once you have this number, to calculate your TDEE, we need to multiply your BMR by your activity level, as outlined in the following chart. If you feel like you're in the middle of one level, choose a number in-between.

ACTIVITY LEVEL	DESCRIPTION	ACTIVITY LEVEL MULTIPLIER
Sedentary	Sitting most of the day, desk job, minimal exercise	BMR x 1.2
Lightly active	Light exercise or sports 1–3 days per week	BMR x 1.375
Moderately active	Moderate exercise or sports 6–7 days per week	BMR x 1.55
Very active	Hard exercise every day	BMR x 1.725
Extra active	Hard exercise 2 or more times per day and/or triathlon/marathon training	BMR x 1.9

Using me as the example again, my BMR was 1903.75, and because I strength train very hard every day, go on multiple dog walks and do lots of incidental walking from A to B, I consider myself Extra Active, so I would do the following calculation to work out my total daily energy expenditure.

1903.75 x 1.9 = 3617.125 (TDEE)

STEP 3

Now that I know my TDEE is 3617.125 per day, I can then calculate my safe calorie deficit.

CALCULATING A SAFE CALORIE DEFICIT

My recommendation for sustainable long-term weight loss that stays off is a calorie deficit of between 500 and 700 calories per day. Your deficit can come from either reducing your food intake, increasing your exercise/activity level or a healthy combination of both, which is exactly what the 5 in 5 plan is.

For your results to be as easy as possible, you'll want to follow the recommended meal plans, stick to and track your daily movement and exercise, and adhere to my advice for eating out and 'cheat' meals so you're as precise as possible. You'll find out more about this as you read on.

If you have a week where you are less active, you may want to look at adjusting your meal quantities, and if you have a very active week, you can either enjoy a bigger deficit to expedite results (as long as you're not hungry) or increase your food intake while maintaining your desired deficit.

THE 5 IN 5 CALORIE DEFICIT EXPLAINED

The weekly meal plans in this book come to a total of 1800 calories per day. For some, you'll want to hit your activity goals to make sure this is a suitable deficit for you, and for others, you'll need to incorporate one or both of the snacks to make sure your deficit isn't too much.

If you can't exercise, you're struggling with an injury or you don't have the ability to stay active, you may find the 1800 calories per day does not put you in enough of a deficit or a deficit at all. This is when you look at removing a side and/or reducing your main meal portions. But as I've already mentioned, I'm not about deprivation, starvation or scarily low benchmarks for daily calories. I'd rather see you eat a plentiful amount of food and be more active, because the benefits of extra movement or exercise, alongside the abundant meals, lead to longer term success, happiness and wellbeing.

To meet your individual goals with ease, be sure to follow the guidelines explained in this book. As your body fat decreases and lean muscle mass increases, your metabolic rate will increase too, so checking your stats and recalibrating your energy requirements is important every 5 weeks.

I have made sure you're getting your daily calories from a healthy variety of protein, fats and carbs. I've said it before and I'll say it again, please don't fear ingredients or food groups I have used in this plan. They are there because they work. They all contribute to balance, flavour, performance and results.

NOT ALL CALORIES ARE CREATED EQUAL

I can't stress this one enough, because a simple scroll online or through social media shows some people stating that it doesn't matter where the calories you consume come from as long as you're hitting your daily needs and staying in a deficit. You'll see people slamming down and/or encouraging fast food, thickshakes and all the chocolate and sweet treats they can devour within their specific calorie needs and claim they are getting the results they want. And look, in theory, yes, 100 calories from a banana is the same as 100 calories from a doughnut, but does that mean we should be eating the doughnut? No, because it comes back to the quality of food being vital, not just the quantity.

Even if the calorie content of a food is the same, the nutrient value of that food won't be. And the nutritional value of the food we eat has a direct link to how we gain, maintain or lose weight. Fast, processed, refined and high-sugar foods tend to lead to hormonal, metabolism, mood, energy and appetite issues. Whereas real, whole and as unrefined as possible foods, cooked from scratch (like the ones in this book) promote increased energy levels, fantastic digestion, improved gut health, satiety and overall better mood and performance.

I refer to junk food as containing 'empty calories', because, while they may hit your energy needs, they don't stack up when it comes to benefiting your health. So, even though in the simplest form, results can be achieved by sticking to a calorie deficit with whatever food you want, it isn't good for us long term, sets us up for health issues and affects our digestion, energy and vitality. I hope you now know why it's so important that in this deficit we are hitting our daily calorie target and macronutrient needs with real food sources. Look at it this way – how you feel and perform after 100 calories of pure refined sugar will certainly be very different from how you feel and perform after 100 calories of quality well-sourced protein.

The 5 in 5 plan isn't just about counting calories. To optimise results, it also considers the nutrient value of those calories and makes sure they're coming from the best possible sources. Do you have any wiggle room on this rule? Well, sort of. Let me explain . . .

Introducing IIFYM (if it fits your macros)

One thing I have found that helps keep people on track is providing flexibility with how they follow my programs and plans. And that's where IIFYM, AKA flexible dieting, comes into play.

IIFYM comes in handy when you're travelling, going out with friends or, for whatever reason, simply need a cheat meal to break up your routine. So, rather than fall completely off the wagon, you allow yourself one cheat meal – or at most one day – per week where you can eat what you want 'if it fits your macros'.

And by that, I mean you're getting your required macronutrients (proteins, fats and carbs) to provide the correct calories for your day, for your specific goal, which includes weight loss. Now, I am fully supportive of this as a sometimes measure if you think it will keep you on track, but it isn't to be used as an excuse to sacrifice nutrient density for convenience or laziness. Because the best, long-term results come from the combination of the quality and quantity of your calories consumed.

I never want you to feel stuck, like you can't go on holidays or socialise, so keep this tool up your sleeve for when life happens and you don't want your goals to get in the way. I use a simple food diary app on my phone (see below), which allows me to search for popular mainstream foods I'm likely to eat out or I can enter them in myself. This kind of tool will help you navigate cheat meals and, within balance and reason, make them a part of your plan.

With all this talk of BMR, TDEE and IIFYM, how do we actually keep track of it all? Read on . . .

HOW DO I MEASURE AND TRACK MY CALORIES AND MACRONUTRIENTS?

Training and nutrition diaries

At the start of any diet or lifestyle change I recommend you have a food and exercise diary. It can be old-school like a basic blank notepad and pen, more professional like a pre-designed fitness diary available in fitness stores or online, or these days what I find easiest is an app. The one I use is My Fitness Pal, which allows me to measure everything I do. It's got features covering my food, exercise, daily schedule and more. It allows me to search for individual ingredients, common recipes, well-known restaurant food and items from supermarkets, providing me with the accurate calorie and macronutrient breakdown. I can also enter in my own recipes to get an accurate count on what I'm consuming. From a fitness perspective, it provides me with suggested workouts, as well as the ability to create my own, with video tutorials, tips and the functionality to track each week's sessions so I know what I performed, how much I lifted, how long I recovered for, and what I need to lift next.

Fitness wearables

I accurately measure my food and exercise with a fitness watch that tracks my heart rate, workouts, sleep and so much more. It counts my steps, records the intensity of my workouts and gives me a fairly accurate look at what I burn in each session, on a dog walk and across the day. I find it gives me peace of mind knowing I am recording what my body expends in calories a day, and when paired with my food diary as mentioned on the previous page, I am as close as possible to understanding my calorie needs for my specific goal.

You can start with something basic like a step counter to keep you accountable to your movement each day or treat yourself to something more advanced to make this a longer term, lifelong commitment.

WHY DOES THE 5 IN 5 WORK?

Studies have consistently shown that people who track their calories, monitor their physical workouts and approach weight loss holistically get results.

When we record our nutrition, training and overall wellness goals, we turn something from simply being an idea into something measurable and achievable, therefore making us accountable. There is a huge difference between an intended thought and a tangible action, and that's why people have such great success following this method.

This process of tracking, monitoring and measuring also gives us great insight into our own habits – when and where we tend to slip up and why, what triggers certain food and lifestyle choices – and the ability to look back and reflect, as well as make plans for what's required to achieve a certain outcome.

It works because you know what you're doing and you're not going into the next 5 weeks blind.

LOSING THE FIRST 5 KG VERSUS THE LAST 5 KG

Often when we start a new diet and healthy lifestyle plan, the results come easily. There are a few factors as to why, but broadly it's due to the following:

- We've been in a very high-calorie surplus, so any reduction to eating makes a big difference.
- We've been eating the wrong types of food, so when we clean up our nutrition, weight comes off more easily.
- We introduce other positive lifestyle factors we weren't doing ordinarily, such as sleeping better, reducing and managing stress and practising self-care.
- We lose excess water retention as exercise and good nutrition open the detoxification pathways.

That's why at the start of a program we feel really motivated and love the process. But it's important we acknowledge the plateaus in the middle of any plan, and the hurdles we face at the end of any wellness journey, especially when it comes to losing those stubborn LAST 5 kilograms.

I hear you, and so many of us have been there. You've stuck to your guns, stayed on track, but no matter what you do, you can't seem to shift any more weight. Here are some of the reasons why you might not be achieving the weight loss you want, and what to do about it:

- **You're overeating.** In the middle and towards the end of any weight-loss program it's easy to begin to slip into old habits, which include portion sizes getting slightly bigger each week, or discretionary snacks sneaking in throughout the day. The best way to combat this is to do a stocktake of your training and nutrition. Return to the principles learned in this book and recalculate and recalibrate your stats so you can get back on track.
- **You've stopped tracking your meals.** Maybe you went on holiday, or had a stressful week at home or work, and, for whatever reason, you stopped tracking your food properly. This is a sure-fire way to lose track of what you're supposed to be having and when. Stop guessing and get back to keeping a journal, and add your workouts in it too. This simple act will bring back the accountability.
- **You're not prepared.** One of the best ways to achieve success when it comes to weight loss is being prepared. That means doing your grocery shop and meal prepping ahead, if need be, and having the right ingredients on hand to make the meals that get results. If you don't, what happens is you end up reaching for convenience foods that don't support your macro or calorie requirements, and before long you're no longer in a deficit and you're no longer getting results. Make a shopping list, cook in bulk, have back-up meals in the freezer and you'll be a few steps closer to getting where you want to be.
- **You're back on the booze.** As a non-drinker of course it's easy for me to harp on about alcohol consumption. But truly, so many times I have watched clients get epic results, only to see them stall in their progress with the reintroduction of booze. Just one glass here or there makes a huge difference to your daily calorie intake, so if you've reached a plateau, take stock of the role alcohol is playing in your life and how it is affecting your health. Alcohol often leads us to make poorer food choices in the moment, so those nachos or that bowl of chips that wouldn't ordinarily be of interest suddenly become a whole lot more tempting when under the influence.
- **You've stopped training and let daily movement and exercise take a back seat in your list of priorities.** Injuries, inclement weather or just a busy schedule can get in the way of moving each day. Sometimes that alarm goes off and the last thing you want to do is get out of bed and exercise, but never forget how much better off you'll be for it. It aids in assisting your energy, boosts your mood and supports your desired calorie deficit while still allowing you to enjoy an abundance of good food. If you really can't exercise or keep your daily movement going, readjust your daily calorie intake accordingly so you remain in that deficit of between 500 and 700 calories.
- **Life is getting the better of you.** That's right, sometimes life feels hard and just sucks. It could be matters of the heart, wallet or home, but, regardless, your emotional state can make a huge difference to your results. Check in with your stress levels, manage any pressures you've got in your life and never forget to give back to yourself. Self-care in hard times is one of the most amazing ways to nurture yourself back to being more in tune with you. Have a massage, go for a big walk in nature, do something you love; it could be just what you need to get back on track.

If in doubt, head to page 39 and read through the 5 in 5 core principles. It's a simple checklist to remind you of the keys to weight-loss success.

WE ARE AL
ONE SMAL
AWAY FRO
STEPPING
POTENTIA

L ONLY
DECISION
M
INTO OUR
.

WHAT ABOUT EXERCISE?

Exercise is a vital component of succeeding with the 5 in 5.

I have designed the recipes and meal plans to not only support and supplement daily movement, but also consider the calories you'll burn each day staying active, so you'll never feel like you're restricted or limited with the types of food, how often or how much you can eat. Yes, you can achieve incredible results from eating good food, but you'll be missing out on so many of the added lifestyle benefits that exercise offers and that really bring the 5 in 5 together.

Exercise improves mood, and when undertaking any lifestyle change, it's important to stay positive because you'll always have ups and downs. Plus, if you've been struggling with your weight for a while, chances are you're not feeling your best, so getting those important endorphins going is crucial to success.

Exercise helps increase your energy. I know the concept of expending energy to gain energy sounds counterintuitive, but when you move, your cardiovascular health improves. As that happens, more oxygen is circulated through your cells, and as you maintain a good movement routine, you end up restocking your mitochondria stores in your body. And mitochondria are what keep you going every day.

Exercise also helps you look good from the inside out. As you get your body moving and your heart rate up, you generate more oxygen and blood pumping through the body. This helps with detoxification and the distribution of nutrients throughout your entire system, and gives you a general overall glow that comes from staying active.

Your results with the 5 in 5 can be accelerated and maintained more easily when regular exercise and daily movement are part of your life. Here's what I'm asking you to do for the next 5 weeks:

- **Minimum 30 minutes of cardiovascular movement 6 days per week:**
  This can be walking, jogging, running, boxing, swimming or group fitness. The key is doing something you enjoy so you're more likely to stick to it. Now, this is a minimum, so feel free to do more if you are fit, willing and able. If 30 structured minutes, 6 days a week isn't your thing, you can swap out this option for a minimum of 10,000 steps per day. Use a fitness tracker or phone app to keep yourself accountable.
- **Minimum 30 minutes of strength-based exercise 3 days per week:**
  On top of your cardiovascular minimums, I am asking you to incorporate strength training into your weekly movement routine. Strength training is where we build, tone and maintain lean muscle. It's vital as we get older to support everyday functional movement and allow us to live pain-free as we age.

For those of you who track your workouts using a fitness wearable, you'll have fairly accurate stats of how many calories you burn in each session and in each day.

Exercise can earn you more food in a day. You can choose to use the extra calories you've burned through exercise as a way to increase the quantity of food you eat in a day, as long as you remain in the recommended calorie deficit of 500–700 calories. Alternatively, if you find your exercise increases your deficit by more than your preferred 500–700 calories, you can keep your eating plan as is to increase the calorie deficit and fast-track your results. If you go for a higher calorie deficit, just make sure you're having adequate amounts of protein to prevent muscle loss and that you always feel energised and fuelled, and never go hungry.

Whether it's cardio, strength, Pilates or yoga, or your goal is to lean up, muscle up or get a strong core, scan the QR code on page 40 for workout ideas for men and women of all fitness levels and abilities.

REST, RECOVERY AND MINDSET

When you're eating right and exercising daily, it's so important to manage your rest, recovery and mindset. Diet and training alone don't create wellbeing. You've got to find synergy between what you fuel your body with, how you move it and how you take care of it. That's why these are non-negotiables for me when it comes to undertaking any lifestyle change.

QUALITY SLEEP

Not getting adequate quality sleep affects all aspects of our lives. We all know how we feel, perform and react when we lack good sleep, and it makes a difference to our results too. When we sleep, we're allowing our digestive system to rest and recover, our muscles to repair and rebuild and our brain to recharge and replenish to face each day. The quality, or lack thereof, of our sleep has a direct impact on how we gain, lose or hold on to excess weight.

Research states that people aged 18 years and above should aim for 7–9 hours' sleep, depending on activity level and lifestyle factors. Ways to improve and increase your sleep quality include daily exercise, limiting caffeine intake after midday, reducing screen time prior to bed, managing stress and reducing/eliminating alcohol.

REDUCE SCREEN TIME

Not only does screen time influence our sleep quality, it also causes issues for our overall wellbeing. If we stay too connected throughout the day, we can experience increased stress levels. This comes down to a number of factors, including feeling like we can never switch off from work, constantly comparing ourselves to others on social media, or mindlessly wasting time scrolling the internet when instead we could be looking after our wellbeing. To help manage and reduce your screen time:

- Perform your daily exercise without your phone, or set your phone to airplane mode so you can't be distracted by calls, emails or social media.
- Spend time outdoors in nature with friends or animals without your phone.
- Manage your notification settings so you can control what interrupts your day and when.
- Make sure you don't use your phone after 8 pm or within 1 hour of bedtime to promote better sleep.
- Unfollow social media accounts that trigger self-esteem issues, make you compare yourself to others, or question your value and current position on your journey in life.

STRESS

At some point in our lives, we all experience stress of some kind. It could be work, family, financial or mental stress that we struggle with. The stress we experience can vary from mild to extreme and has a direct impact on how we live our lives each day. Recent statistics have shown that 72 per cent of Aussies feel that stress affects their physical health, with 64 per cent of respondents saying it affects their mental health. And they're right. Stress has a flow-on effect to the foods we choose, whether we commit to exercise or not, and how we manage our time so we get adequate sleep. Daily exercise has an incredible impact on helping us to manage our stress better, along with daily mindfulness, gratitude practice, meditation and connecting with others. When following the 5 in 5, the food and movement plan will help you to manage your stress, but don't forget these other techniques if you're feeling overwhelmed.

STRETCH

Stretching is not everyone's cup of tea, but hear me out. I, like many, don't love stretching, for a few reasons: at times I find it tedious, at others I find it difficult because I'm feeling quite tight. But what really helps me overcome the hurdle of incorporating stretching into my daily life is combining it with some of the above-mentioned tools and techniques for managing stress. And because I'm achieving a few things at once, not only am I winning at time management, but I've also found a life hack to keep on top of my stress and my recovery.

When I stretch, I see it as time to be both screen-free and mindful. I disconnect from life's distractions, am present in the moment and allow my mind to be free of any control, letting my thoughts come and go as they please, without holding on to anything. Plus, the act of stretching lengthens my muscles after they've been tightened by exercise, and the result is a supple, agile, pain-free post-workout feeling with a clear mind and positive outlook. If you really want to win at self-care, try repeating positive mantras as you hold each stretch, such as 'I am worthy, I am well, I am where I am supposed to be'.

THE 5 IN 5 EATING PLAN

The best way to describe the 5 in 5 eating plan is as a real wholefood-based diet that celebrates a healthy balance of protein, fat and carbs in a way that gives you plenty of variety, while maximising results, without making you feel like you're eliminating food groups or missing out.

And the best part is, each and every recipe requires only 5 core ingredients or fewer. That means you only need a handful of items to create a week's worth of mouth-watering breakfasts, lunches, dinners and snacks that really satisfy. You'll save on time (less shopping, less prep), foster a better connection with food, nutrition and cooking habits, and create fuss-free meals every day that will get you closer to your goals.

RECIPE SYMBOL EXPLAINER

All the recipes in this book fall into the following categories. You'll see these symbols with each recipe, so you'll know at a glance just what the nutritional properties are. If the symbol has an asterisk, the recipe can be tweaked slightly with a simple swap to make it fit that category – simply read the intro, ingredients list or the pro tip on how it can be done.

Please, regardless of where you currently sit on the food spectrum, do not be scared of a specific food group or way of eating. Although you may have dietary or personal preferences, studies have shown that weight loss always comes down to the calories consumed and expended, and whether the deficit came from low-carb, keto, high-protein, carnivore or plant-based foods made no difference in overall results. But if following a certain style or way of eating makes you feel great, function better, or is just a personal preference overall, it may assist you to achieve a calorie deficit. Make adjustments, if need be – some of which I have shared below and on page 33 to help tailor this plan to your needs for optimal success.

DF: Dairy Free

Like gluten, some people can have an inflammatory response to dairy; in particular lactose, a sugar found in dairy. I've made this book safe for those of you who are lactose intolerant or simply don't enjoy high amounts of dairy, with the occasional exception of high-quality unsweetened plain yoghurt, which can be substituted with unsweetened plain coconut yoghurt. Grass-fed butter, which is made from milk fat and protein and contains negligible traces of lactose, can be swapped for the same quantity of extra-virgin olive oil or coconut oil. If you choose to eat dairy, make sure it's high quality, high welfare and, if possible, organic. Cheese is used sparingly in some recipes – if you're dairy free, it can be omitted or swapped for a plant-based alternative.

GF: Gluten Free

Gluten can cause inflammation in some individuals, which manifests, among other reactions, as issues with their digestion and gut health. As a rule, I like to keep all my recipes gluten free so everyone can enjoy them. This book is 100 per cent gluten free bar the occasional use of gluten-free rolled oats, which come with their own caveat – please see page 30.

LC: Low Carb

Lots of recipes in this book are low carb and avoid higher carb starchy ingredients. When we reduce the carbs on our plate, the rest of the meal can be made up of quality protein and healthy fats, which in turn keep us feeling fuller for longer. I implement lower carb recipes to help manage satiety levels throughout the 5 weeks, while still celebrating good-quality well-sourced carbs to keep you energised each day.

PB: Plant Based

If a recipe is marked as plant based, it will be free from any animal products and is suitable for vegans and vegetarians. Animal proteins can be subbed with plant-based alternatives such as tofu or tempeh if the cooking process is suitable. If a recipe calls for eggs, they can in most cases be replaced with flax or chia eggs. Please be advised, though, you'll have to adjust the calories for any changes you make when tweaking recipes to suit your diet or lifestyle.

RSF: Refined-sugar Free

The recipes in this book are predominantly refined-sugar free. All ingredients have natural sugars – even a low-carb vegetable like broccoli contains fructose, glucose, sucrose and tiny amounts of lactose and maltose – which means most recipes include sugar in some form and we can't avoid it completely. My recipes avoid any added, refined or processed sugars. The refined-sugar-free sweeteners I use in this book are pure maple syrup, raw honey and coconut sugar. You can use monk fruit sweetener to make my recipes lower carb and/or keto friendly; please see page 30 for more on this.

A NOTE ON GLUTEN

A small number of recipes in this book call for rolled oats labelled as gluten free (or wheat free). Pure oats are gluten free; often it is the machinery they are processed with that contaminates them. If using, please always select certified gluten-free (or wheat-free) rolled oats to avoid cross-contamination from processing. Gluten-free rolled oats are suitable for those who choose to avoid gluten-containing products but do not have any specific health issue. If, however, you are in any way sensitive, intolerant or allergic to gluten, especially if you have coeliac disease, you should only consume oats under the advice, support and guidance of your health professional, as avenin, the protein in oats, can cause inflammation and long-term damage.

A NOTE ON SWEETENERS

Any time a recipe calls for maple syrup or honey, you can reduce the calories and carbs of that dish by using monk fruit sweetener, which comes in both a liquid and granule form, with a variety of different flavour profiles – I like using the brand Lakanto. In this book, when a recipe calls for maple syrup or honey, I recommend using Lakanto maple-flavoured syrup or golden malt syrup. If a recipe calls for granulated coconut sugar, I recommend Lakanto classic, golden or baking blend varieties. These are all readily available in supermarkets, health-food stores, online health retailers and my own online store. They are a 1:1 sugar replacement, suitable for diabetics and are zero glycaemic, so are another tool to equip you for success.

PROTEIN: WHY IS IT IMPORTANT?

I can't stress enough the importance of protein. It's a crucial macronutrient when it comes to losing body fat, building and maintaining lean muscle mass, and feeling fuller for longer. High-protein meals and snacks can reduce our cravings for poorer food choices and keep us satiated between meals, preventing us from falling off track.

If you are looking specifically to maintain or build muscle mass, you'll want to make sure you get the right amount of protein per day. Much like calories, your protein intake required to gain lean muscle mass will vary based on age, fitness level and types of training you do. But for a bulking phase, I recommend 2 g of protein per 1 kg of body weight. So, if you're 80 kg, 80 x 2 = 160 g protein per day. And that doesn't mean a 160 g piece of chicken, it means the total protein found from your food across the day. Chicken breast, for example, contains 33 g of protein per 100 g serve. Once you're happy with your size, a more manageable maintenance phase is 1.5 g protein per kg of body weight.

MEAL PLAN STRUCTURE EXPLAINER

In the 5 weeks of meal plans, I have created a core layout of breakfasts, lunches, dinners and sides that total between 1700 and 1800 calories or as close to, give or take, per day. This will have most people in a safe calorie deficit when taking into account the weekly exercise recommended on the 5 in 5 plan. Under these core meals, there is the addition of two snacks that are designed for people who have highly active lifestyles, exercise strenuously, or need excess calories to make sure they aren't in too much of a deficit, or want to revert to a maintenance or surplus phase. For those wanting to maintain or build lean muscle mass, you'll want to incorporate these snacks to support your training goals and prevent muscle wastage. The side dish each day can be paired with any of the main meals, or enjoyed between main meals as a snack. Alternatively, you can swap the side for one of the drinks or sweet snacks if you prefer. If you do not consider yourself active or are unable to adhere to the 5 in 5 movement plan, please omit the side altogether, to keep you in a suitable calorie deficit for optimal results.

BREAKFAST	For all
LUNCH	For all
DINNER	For all
SIDE	Optional (have any time of day or swap for a drink or sweet snack)
SNACK #1	Optional for those needing extra calories for active lifestyle
SNACK #2	Optional for men or active women wanting to increase lean muscle mass on maintenance or surplus calories

ARE THE RECIPES INTERCHANGEABLE?

I have designed the meal plans in a way that offers variety, minimises wastage and tries to use similar ingredients within each week to make it cost effective. If a recipe serves 2 or 4, I either use the multiple serves across the week, or recommend storing leftovers in the freezer for future use. On the meal plan it'll say to eat one serve, keep one serve in the fridge for the next day or freeze leftover serves for later.

If you aren't a fan of a particular type of recipe, ingredient or flavour combination, please feel free to swap out and adjust accordingly. Choose a recipe with a similar number of calories so your daily calorie intake stays on track.

CAN WE DO THIS AS A FAMILY?

Yes, absolutely. You can do this solo, with a friend or housemate, or with the entire family. Just multiply the recipes according to how many serves you require to feed the mouths in your home, being mindful that if someone has a more active lifestyle or higher daily calorie need, they'll need bigger serves or extra snacks.

The meals are well rounded, balanced and offer a fantastic variety of macros and micronutrients, and are suitable for all ages and lifestyles. Although the food is very safe for the whole family to consume, please don't implement the exercise specifications for under 18s, especially young children.

Note: if you have any specific dietary requirement, allergen or health condition, it's important to consult a health professional before changing anything in your diet or lifestyle and get the advice that's right for you.

WHAT ABOUT SNACKING?

Snacks are an important part of the 5 in 5 and that's why I've created a delicious Treats chapter. These recipes not only taste great, but are healthy alternatives to ordinary fast or convenience foods. They take away that craving for something that would derail your goals, while still being yummy and a little bit cheeky.

If you're hungry, it's handy to make bulk snacks and keep single portions in the fridge and freezer so you always have something healthy to reach for.

As explained in the meal plan section, more snacks can be incorporated depending on your daily energy requirements and goals. Your daily side dish can be utilised as a snack and enjoyed any time of day or swapped for one of the optional sweet snacks.

CAN I EAT OUT/GET TAKEAWAY?

Yes, but don't make a habit of it. I still want you to live your life, so, if you're celebrating a special occasion, catching up with friends or simply don't have time to cook for yourself, get takeaway and follow my advice on page 21 about IIFYM and flexible dieting. Be smart about what you order, prioritise protein and veggies, and limit heavy, oily or processed foods. These days, healthier options can be found almost everywhere.

WHAT IF I'M TRAVELLING?

Much like with takeaway, life should always come first, and whether it's for work or pleasure, some of us live lives on the go. You can still achieve incredible results by following the meal plans as best as you possibly can when home in your own kitchen, and then follow my IIFYM flexible eating advice while on the road. When I travel, I pack my own snacks to eat on planes, research healthy restaurants and cafes at my destination, and try to find accommodation with cooking facilities so I'm in control of what I eat.

WHAT IF I'M HUNGRY/TOO FULL?

Feeling hungry all the time could be a sign that you're not having enough calories in your day. The meal plans are designed to keep you satiated, but if you're extremely active, train hard or perform lots of incidental exercise, then you may need to increase your portions or snacks throughout the day. Sometimes dehydration is mistaken for hunger, so be sure to keep on top of your water needs each day. This is explained in more detail on the opposite page.

Conversely, if you're feeling full before you've finished your meals, don't force yourself to finish them. Keep any leftovers in an airtight container in the fridge for later or another day. It's about being intuitive enough to eat when you're genuinely hungry and stop when you're feeling full.

Just be mindful when adding or subtracting calories from a day if you eat more or less, because eating less one day will reduce your calorie intake, and then enjoying leftovers on top of another day's food can increase that day's calories. As long as you're not over- or under-eating every day, it should balance out. If you eat what's designated for your week – even if that means eating it on different days – you will still achieve the desired results. It's more the extremes on either end of the spectrum we need to be mindful of.

HOW MUCH HYDRATION?

Up to 80 per cent of the human body is made up of water, so it's no surprise how important it is to stay hydrated for optimal health and results when doing the 5 in 5. It is vital for digestion, absorption, detoxification and the regulation of our temperature and bodily functions. We get one-fifth of our water needs from the food and fluids we ingest, meaning we need to source the remainder from clean, pure water. Generally speaking, the average woman requires 2 litres (8 cups) of water per day, and the average man needs 2.5 litres (10 cups) per day. This doesn't take into account exerting ourselves through physical activity, being in a hot environment, or consuming high amounts of diuretics. So, increase your fluid intake accordingly to account for lifestyle factors. Keep a reusable water bottle on you to help you stay on track.

Signs you're not getting enough water include tiredness, lack of focus, irritability and particularly yellow/dark urine. These are good indications you need to take a big sip. Secondly, sometimes dehydration is mistaken for hunger. So, instead of instantly reaching for more food, have a glass of water and wait 30 minutes; in most cases, that feeling of hunger will subside.

WHAT ABOUT TWEAKING?

You can adapt and adjust the 5 in 5 to suit your preferred diet or lifestyle. Some people prefer to eat a certain way and believe they will feel better or get better results if they stick to that. And I completely respect you doing what you need to do to make this work for you. I can assure you the plan I have mapped out works, but if you want to make tweaks, here's how:

Fasting

Intermittent fasting works wonderfully in conjunction with the 5 in 5. Time your meals according to your preferred fasting regime (12:12/16:8/18:6) and adjust the serving sizes if you need to fit more or less macros in a specific eating window.

High healthy fat

Reduce the carb and protein portions in each meal and increase the healthy fats by adding more extra-virgin olive oil while cooking, and adding avocados, nuts, seeds and olives.

High protein

Decrease the carbs and fat in a recipe and add extra protein. Swap out any higher carb meals for higher protein meals in the meal plan.

Low carb/keto

Replace below-ground root vegetables, such as potato and sweet potato, with pumpkin. Replace gluten-free pasta or rice with zucchini noodles, konjac noodles, cauliflower rice or konjac rice. Swap out higher sugar fruits, like bananas, for low-fructose fruits like berries.

Plant based/vegan

Swap out animal proteins for your preferred plant-based alternative if the cooking style is suitable. Replace butter with extra-virgin olive oil or coconut oil, cheese with a dairy-free substitute and yoghurt with a dairy-free coconut variety.

THE TAKEAWAY HERE

Regardless of how you adjust and adapt the program to suit you and your lifestyle, the key is tracking your calories, so you still hit your target, and adjusting each meal's macros according to the changes you make to it. That's why having a fitness wearable and meal planner/calorie tracker app come in handy. The fact is, as long as you are in the required calorie deficit, you will still achieve results. Just make sure you hit your macros from quality sources.

SHOULD I WEIGH MYSELF AND WHEN?

Weighing yourself is an important part of the 5 in 5 if you're following your calories closely. Not only do you need your current weight to calculate your ideal calorie deficit, but you will want to weigh yourself either once a week or at the end of the 5 weeks to track your results. Your weight will be an indicator of how well you're progressing and if anything needs tightening up or adjusting to achieve 5 in 5 success.

What I don't want you to do is weigh yourself daily. This is counterintuitive and can mess with your head. Because, depending on what you've eaten, time of day, fluid retention or whether you have passed any stools that day, your weight can fluctuate dramatically, which is why it should be once per week or, at a minimum, at the start and at the end of the plan.

Here is how to weigh yourself for accurate results:

- Weigh yourself first thing upon waking, preferably at the same time each week.
- Go to the toilet, if you need to, prior to weighing yourself.
- Wear as little clothing as possible – or none – and make sure you're in the same thing each time.
- Be barefoot, with your feet evenly distributed and the scales on a hard flat surface.

I don't want you to become obsessed or disheartened with the weighing process. And please don't freak out or give up if the numbers don't go in your favour. There is a chance you've lost body fat and increased lean muscle mass, you may be constipated or holding on to fluid, or you simply may have hit a plateau as outlined on page 22. Beyond the numbers on the scale, check in with how you're feeling, how much energy you have, how your clothes are fitting and how you feel when looking at yourself in the mirror. These are all equally important measures for feeling confident in the skin you're in.

BEFORE AND AFTER PHOTOS

Before and after photos are a really fantastic way to measure results, stay on track and remind yourself of how far you've come. We often forget where we started, and seeing what we looked like then can be a nice way to realise how hard we've worked and how good our results actually are. You don't have to show anyone your pics, they can be completely personal. Or you can share them publicly as a way of staying accountable (like I did). Regardless, here is how to take the perfect before and after progress photos:

SHOW YOUR SHAPE

Be brave enough to be vulnerable, especially with the before. You need to wear something fitted and/or revealing to show the true state of your shape at each stage of the journey. Fitted active wear or swimwear that shows plenty of skin is a good starting point. Avoid loose-fitting or baggy outfits that hide definition.

SAME OR A SIMILAR OUTFIT

It's good to compare where you started with how far you've come in the same or a similar outfit. This gives a gauge of how it fits differently and how your new body wears this same style.

LOCATION, LOCATION, LOCATION

Choose the same blank wall, in a well-lit location, without any backlight. Having a clear blank canvas of sorts behind you brings the focus back to you, and the more well-lit, the better – so you can see yourself properly. I like a plain white or black wall, with natural or halo light, if possible, without any light or windows behind me.

ANGLES

Get help from a friend or loved one, or even use a tripod with self-timer mode on your camera. You want to get front, back and side angles, taken from the same angle, showing your whole body. Make sure you are centre of frame, and don't cut off any limbs or your head.

I know it may feel confronting at first, but you'll thank me. Often, it's hard to see the changes as they happen each day, and it's only once you look back and compare that you can truly appreciate how far you've come and the great results you've achieved.

YOU ARE L
BEYOND M
YOU ARE M
WORTHY T
EVER KNO
DESERVE T

VED
EASURE,
ORE
HAN YOU'LL
V, AND YOU
HIS.

WHAT HAPPENS AFTER THE FIRST 5 WEEKS?

Firstly, congratulations for sticking to the 5 in 5. That, in itself, is a great achievement. Give yourself a massive pat on the back for your progress so far. But what's next?

Do your weigh-in and look at your before and after photos, then sit back and decide for yourself.

Do I have more weight to lose?

If so, recalculate your new BMR and TDEE (as outlined on page 19) to find the correct calorie deficit and get started on another 5-week round.

Am I happy with the weight I am now?

If so, recalculate your new BMR and TDEE (as outlined on page 19) and adjust your food intake for maintenance calories.

Would I like to gain some lean muscle mass?

If you'd like to add some lean muscle mass size in conjunction with adequate strength training, and in some cases, bulk up, recalculate your BMR and TDEE (as outlined on page 19) and calculate your calorie surplus. I recommend between 300 and 500 calories extra per day for lean muscle gain, while minimising extra fat storage.

Do I want to transition to intuitive eating?

These first 5 weeks may have taught you enough about taking your health into your own hands that you want to become an intuitive eater. This is when you can stop counting calories and tap more into how you feel, keeping in mind the principles around intuitive eating outlined on page 17.

FIVE IN FIVE

THE 5 IN 5 CORE PRINCIPLES

- FOLLOW THE MEAL PLANS
- STAY HYDRATED WITH A MINIMUM OF 2 LITRES OF WATER PER DAY
- 30 MINUTES OF CARDIOVASCULAR EXERCISE 6 DAYS PER WEEK OR 10,000 STEPS DAILY
- 30 MINUTES OF STRENGTH TRAINING 3 DAYS PER WEEK
- NO ALCOHOL
- MINIMUM OF 7–9 HOURS' SLEEP DAILY
- DEDICATED SCREEN-FREE TIME
- STRETCH
- PRACTISE MINDFULNESS OR MEDITATION
- BACK YOURSELF
- LOVE YOURSELF

A FINAL WORD (PEP TALK) FROM ME

You are loved beyond measure, you are more worthy than you'll ever know, and you deserve this.

Sometimes you just need to put YOU first. You cannot pour from an empty cup, and at some point, something's gotta give, and you've got to give back to you.

Do this program for you, stick to it because you know how good you'll feel when you complete it, and never, ever give up on being the version of you that you were born to be.

Quit the excuses, throw out that negative internal voice, and every day you wake up, be your biggest cheerleader, not your worst critic. You've got this.

Luke xx

For my recommended ingredients, workout ideas, mindset and motivation, scan this QR code to access the ultimate 5 in 5 online support guide and community. Connect with others following the plan, discover new and exciting ingredients, put your plans into action and get any assistance you need.

REFERENCES

How and why do we put on weight?

POOR-QUALITY OR LACK OF SLEEP

Hanlon EC, Tasali E, Leproult R, Stuhr KL, Doncheck E, de Wit H, Hillard CJ, Van Cauter E. 'Sleep Restriction Enhances the Daily Rhythm of Circulating Levels of Endocannabinoid 2-Arachidonoylglycerol'. *Sleep*. 2016 Mar 1; 39(3):653–64. doi: 10.5665/sleep.5546. PMID: 26612385; PMCID: PMC4763355.

STRESS

Bhutani S, Howard JD, Reynolds R, Zee PC, Gottfried J, Kahnt T. 'Olfactory connectivity mediates sleep-dependent food choices in humans'. *eLife*. 2019 Oct 8; 8:e49053. doi: 10.7554/eLife.49053. PMID: 31591965; PMCID: PMC6783266.

Calorie intake, a closer look

CALORIE DEFICIT

Carels RA, Young KM, Coit C, Clayton AM, Spencer A, Hobbs M. 'Can following the caloric restriction recommendations from the Dietary Guidelines for Americans help individuals lose weight?' *Eating Behaviors*. 2008 Aug; 9(3):328–35. doi: 10.1016/j.eatbeh.2007.12.003. Epub 2008 Jan 4. PMID: 18549992.

Why does the 5 in 5 work?

Carels RA, Young KM, Coit C, Clayton AM, Spencer A, Hobbs M. 'Can following the caloric restriction recommendations from the Dietary Guidelines for Americans help individuals lose weight?' *Eating Behaviors*. 2008 Aug; 9(3):328–35. doi: 10.1016/j.eatbeh.2007.12.003. Epub 2008 Jan 4. PMID: 18549992.

Rest, recovery and mindset

QUALITY SLEEP

Watson NF, Badr MS, Belenky G, Bliwise DL, Buxton OM, Buysse D, Dinges DF, Gangwisch J, Grandner MA, Kushida C, Malhotra RK, Martin JL, Patel SR, Quan SF, Tasali E. 'Recommended Amount of Sleep for a Healthy Adult: A Joint Consensus Statement of the American Academy of Sleep Medicine and Sleep Research Society'. *Sleep*. 2015 Jun 1; 38(6):843–4. doi: 10.5665/sleep.4716. PMID: 26039963; PMCID: PMC4434546.

STRESS

Australian Psychological Society. 'Stress & Wellbeing: How Australians are coping with life'. 2015. https://psychology.org.au/getmedia/ae32e645-a4f0-4f7c-b3ce-dfd83237c281/stress-wellbeing-survey.pdf

The 5 in 5 eating plan

RECIPE SYMBOL EXPLAINER

Sacks FM, Bray GA, Carey VJ, Smith SR, Ryan DH, Anton SD, McManus K, Champagne CM, Bishop LM, Laranjo N, Leboff MS, Rood JC, de Jonge L, Greenway FL, Loria CM, Obarzanek E, Williamson DA. 'Comparison of weight-loss diets with different compositions of fat, protein, and carbohydrates'. *New England Journal of Medicine*. 2009 Feb 26; 360(9):859-73. doi: 10.1056/NEJMoa0804748. PMID: 19246357; PMCID: PMC2763382.

5 IN 5 RECIPES EXPLAINER

One of the biggest roadblocks people encounter when trying to make a positive change to their food, nutrition and cooking habits is that recipes are too complicated, time consuming or contain way too many ingredients. Well, let me tell you, with the 5 in 5 eating plan I have removed these obstacles, and therefore excuses, which can sometimes derail the best of intentions. Here's how I have created the recipes for you and why:

5 CORE INGREDIENTS

Each and every recipe contains a maximum of 5 core ingredients. That's right, 5! But what do I mean by core ingredients? These are food items that you may need to buy on top of some healthy everyday gluten-free pantry staples, which I'll introduce you to next. Because the recipes contain only 5 key ingredients or fewer, the drinks, meals, snacks and treats you'll prepare on the 5 in 5 eating plan are less complicated, a breeze to put together and they'll save you money per serve as there is nothing unnecessary and the quantities are designed to minimise wastage.

EASY

Even on the busiest days and nights, when the stress of life takes over, the 5 in 5 meals are incredibly simple and realistic to achieve. Featuring a minimum of nutrient-dense real foods that are easy to buy from your local supermarket or grocer, and with flavours you'd expect from far more intricate dishes, these recipes are all about making the core ingredients shine. Whether you're already a pro in the kitchen or have only recently found your confidence with a spatula, this is the easiest cookbook you'll ever use.

SPEEDY

I want you to spend your time on getting great results and feeling good, not hours slaving away unnecessarily in the kitchen. With my recipes you don't need to soak, marinate or prepare anything the night before, or even for more than 15 minutes. And because the recipes are so fast, you'll have more time to hit the gym, go for a walk, meditate or get some quality sleep.

PLEASE NOTE: All oven temperatures stated are fan-forced, so if you have a conventional oven, you'll need to increase the temperature by about 20°C and be aware that cooking times may vary slightly depending on your oven.

FIVE IN FIVE

5 IN 5 PANTRY STAPLES

Say hello to your 5 in 5 pantry staples.

Along with the 5 core ingredients you'll need for each recipe, some call for the addition of healthy pantry staples. Hopefully, you'll already have most of these on hand, but if not, they're all standard food items that can be found anywhere you buy your groceries. I recommend stocking up on these staples the week before you start your 5 in 5 eating plan to fill any gaps in your pantry. Take a closer look at each one and my helpful tips and swaps for allergies or intolerances.

PLEASE NOTE: Every recipe includes 'next level it' ideas. These are my bonus tidbits about what extra everyday ingredients you can add to elevate the dish. Additional herbs, spices or citrus won't change the overall calories, but calories can creep up when adding nuts, seeds or other key elements. It's always best to use an app to track any changes to your daily calories.

Good oils

- Extra-virgin olive oil
- Coconut oil

Many of my recipes require extra-virgin olive oil or coconut oil. You'll use the extra-virgin olive oil for all your roasting, frying, grilling and dressings, while the coconut oil is predominantly used for desserts.

Water

- Filtered water
- Ice cubes

You'll use filtered water and ice cubes throughout the book in numerous recipes, perhaps to add to a sauce or smoothie. Water plays such an integral part in our health, so it is crucial that the water we drink, use in recipes or make ice with is of the highest quality. Filtered water is free of any odours, chlorine, pesticides, chemicals, heavy metals and bacterial contaminants, making it nothing but delicious, clean, hydrating goodness.

Gluten-free baking powder

One little container will go a long way – well beyond your 5 in 5 – as recipes don't need much. The reason I specify gluten free is sometimes brands add fillers, such as wheat flour, so just read the label closely and look for the 100% gluten-free health claim.

Herbs

- Dried parsley

Dried herbs last for ages, and having a variety in your pantry is a game changer. As a minimum I want you to have some dried parsley; and if possible, I recommend adding dried rosemary and thyme. I am a massive fan of fresh herbs too, and you'll sometimes see in my 'next level it' tips a suggestion to add them to bring colour and life to a dish, but that's only if you really want to, or already have them on hand.

Salt and pepper

- Good-quality rock or sea salt
- Freshly ground black pepper

High-quality simple seasonings elevate recipes to the next level, and apart from some desserts and drinks, most of my recipes require a pinch of salt and pepper. I prefer sea and rock salt over table salt as they are less processed and contain more minerals. And nothing beats the freshness and spice hit of peppercorns just cracked from a grinder.

Spices

- Chilli flakes

I want you to have great-quality chilli flakes on hand, because of the way you can use them in numerous cuisines and their inimitable ability to add oomph and flavour with only a pinch. This is only a start, though; if your budget allows, please load up your spice cupboard with lots of other options, such as smoked paprika, ground cumin and ground coriander.

Flours

- Tapioca flour
- Almond flour

These two gluten-free flours are the base for recipes that traditionally require plain or self-raising refined wheat flour. I've chosen these as both are free of gluten and are great for hitting macro requirements. They can be subbed with a standard gluten-free flour if you prefer.

Acids

- Lemon or lime juice

The acid from citrus helps balance out flavour in many types of food and on occasion a recipe calls for the juice of a lemon or lime. Both can be used in their fresh form or the long-lasting pre-bottled varieties from supermarkets, which are a convenient and cost-effective way of always having some on hand. If you don't have any lemons or limes, apple cider vinegar is a good substitute.

THE 5 IN 5
ABOUT DE
STARVATIO
LIMITATION
EDUCATION
AND FREE

S NOT
RIVATION,
N OR
IT'S ABOUT
EXPANSION
OM.

MEAL PLANS EXPLAINER

To make your 5 in 5 eating plan as easy to follow as possible, I have created 5 weeks of meals following these parameters:

Similar ingredients: You'll see similar ingredients across a 7-day period, such as the same types of veg, protein cuts and store-bought sauces or flavourings. While making shopping easier, this also ensures you use what you buy and minimises wastage.

Repeat meals: I repeat certain meals throughout a week or fortnight to maximise recipes that lend themselves to being cooked in larger quantities. This saves you time in the kitchen because one night's cooking will give you lunches and dinners to enjoy over the following days.

Same meals for everyone: Whether it's your loved one, sibling or housemate, the meal plans are designed to suit both men and women. It's the quantity of snacks in a single day that differentiates the calories for men and women. So, take a close look at your TDEE and the suggested recipes and adjust according to your individual needs, goals and preferences.

Bulk snacks: You'll see snacks are often repeated across the 5 weeks based on how many serves they make. When you prepare a snack in bulk, please divide into the recommended single-serve portions and store in the fridge or freezer for later enjoyment. You can swap any of the snacks around depending on your personal preferences – just keep them within your calorie goals.

Swaps: I totally understand some people don't like a certain type of veg, protein or flavour combo, which is why you can absolutely swap a meal out and replace it with another recipe you love from this book, or with leftovers from a previous meal you made in bulk. Just be mindful to choose something within the same calorie range so you hit your daily target.

Sides: The daily side dish can be enjoyed with any of that day's main meals or between main meals as a snack. This side dish is optional and designed for those who adhere to the 5 in 5 movement protocol. If you consider yourself inactive or are unable to move daily, please omit this side to ensure you remain in a suitable calorie deficit. If you prefer, you can swap these savoury sides for one of the sweet snacks, as long as they are of a similar calorie value. If you're feeling full on the meal plan, the side should be the first thing to be removed, and if you're short on time, the side can be swapped for a smoothie to be enjoyed any time throughout the day.

Base meals for all

Set between 1700 and 1800 calories per day

Optional for active people, to be enjoyed any time of day

FIVE IN FIVE

MEAL PLAN 1

	MONDAY	TUESDAY	WEDNESDAY	THURSDAY	FRIDAY	SATURDAY	SUNDAY
BREAKFAST							
LUNCH							
DINNER							
SIDE							
SNACK #1							
SNACK #2							

Snack for men, or active women, to reach daily calorie target

Snack for extra calories based on goal or activity level

FIVE IN FIVE

MEAL PLAN 1

	MONDAY	TUESDAY	WEDNESDAY
BREAKFAST	Overnight Protein Oats, p. 76 (453 cals)	Caramelised Banana & Cinnamon Porridge, p. 70 (356 cals)	Golden Granola Clusters, p. 74 (472 cals)
LUNCH	Smashed Salmon Salad, p. 116 (555 cals)	Smashed Salmon Salad, p. 116 (555 cals) (Leftovers)	One-pan Harissa Chicken, p. 146 (587 cals) (Leftovers)
DINNER	Classic Steak Frites, p. 159 (493 cals)	One-pan Harissa Chicken, p. 146 (587 cals)	Spicy Spag Meatballs, p. 160 (553 cals)
SIDE	Ultimate Green Salad, p. 106 (328 cals)	Ultimate Green Salad, p. 106 (328 cals) (Leftovers)	Salty Charred Greens, p. 112 (196 cals)

SNACK #1	One-bowl Banana Bread, p. 170 (347 cals)	Black Forest Brownie, p. 179 (263 cals)	Bangin' Bounty-licious Bar, p. 182 (290 cals)
SNACK #2	Choc Peanut Butter Cookie, p. 173 (200 cals)	Carrot Cake Muffin, p. 185 (291 cals)	No-bake Banoffee Slice, p. 176 (317 cals)

MEAL PLAN

1

THURSDAY	FRIDAY	SATURDAY	SUNDAY
Sweet Potato Omelette, p. 82 (440 cals)	Golden Granola Clusters, p. 74 (472 cals) (Leftovers)	Sticky Strawberry Protein Pancakes, p. 73 (572 cals)	Golden Granola Clusters, p. 74 (472 cals) (Leftovers)
Spicy Spag Meatballs, p. 160 (553 cals) (Leftovers)	Indian-spiced Ocean Trout, p. 128 (388 cals) (Leftovers)	Sweet Potato Omelette, p. 82 (440 cals) (Leftovers)	Schnitty & Slaw, p. 139 (683 cals) (Leftovers)
Indian-spiced Ocean Trout, p. 128 (388 cals)	Chicken Satay Burger, p. 142 (558 cals)	Schnitty & Slaw, p. 139 (683 cals)	Thai-style Fish Cakes, p. 122 (346 cals) (Makes 4 serves)
Crispy Mexican Corn Ribs, p. 111 (384 cals)	Crispy Mexican Corn Ribs, p. 111 (384 cals) (Leftovers)	Salty Charred Greens, p. 112 (196 cals) (Leftovers)	Crispy Pumpkin Salad, p. 93 (261 cals)

One-bowl Banana Bread, p. 170 (347 cals) (Leftovers)	Black Forest Brownie, p. 179 (263 cals)	Bangin' Bounty-licious Bar, p. 182 (290 cals)	One-bowl Banana Bread, p. 170 (347 cals) (Leftovers)
Choc Peanut Butter Cookie, p. 173 (200 cals)	Carrot Cake Muffin, p. 185 (291 cals)	No-bake Banoffee Slice, p. 176 (317 cals)	Choc Peanut Butter Cookie, p. 173 (200 cals)

FIVE IN FIVE

MEAL PLAN 2

	MONDAY	TUESDAY	WEDNESDAY
BREAKFAST	Garlicky Hash Browns, p. 88 (586 cals)	Garlicky Hash Browns, p. 88 (586 cals) (Leftovers)	Golden Granola Clusters, p. 74 (472 cals) (Leftovers) ADD 1 sliced banana
LUNCH	Thai-style Fish Cakes, p. 122 (346 cals) (Leftovers)	Spicy Spag Meatballs, p. 160 (553 cals) (Leftovers)	Butter Chicken Bow, p. 134 (388 cals) (Leftovers)
DINNER	Spicy Spag Meatballs, p. 160 (553 cals)	Butter Chicken Bow, p. 134 (388 cals) (Eat 1, keep 1, freeze 2)	Lukey's Lamb Pizza, p. 166 (609 cals)
SIDE	Crispy Pumpkin Salad, p. 93 (261 cals) (Leftovers)	Chilli Charred Cabbage, p. 94 (185 cals)	Chilli Charred Cabbage, p. 94 (185 cals) (Leftovers)
SNACK #1	One-bowl Banana Bread, p. 170 (347 cals)	Black Forest Brownie, p. 179 (263 cals)	Bangin' Bounty-licious Bar, p. 182 (290 cals)
SNACK #2	Choc Peanut Butter Cookie, p. 173 (200 cals)	Carrot Cake Muffin, p. 185 (291 cals)	No-bake Banoffee Slice, p. 176 (317 cals)

MEAL PLAN

2

THURSDAY	FRIDAY	SATURDAY	SUNDAY
Overnight Protein Oats, p. 76 (453 cals)	Pineapple Colada Smoothie, p. 62 (306 cals)	Crispy Pumpkin Fritters, p. 85 (502 cals)	Crispy Pumpkin Fritters, p. 85 (502 cals) (Leftovers)
Lukey's Lamb Pizza, p. 166 (609 cals) (Leftovers)	One-pan Tuna Pasta Bake, p. 120 (514 cals) (Leftovers)	Fish 'n' Fries in a Flash, p. 125 (504 cals) (Leftovers)	Spicy Beef Tacos, p. 162 (371 cals) (Leftovers)
One-pan Tuna Pasta Bake, p. 120 (514 cals) (Eat 1, keep 1, freeze 2)	Fish 'n' Fries in a Flash, p. 125 (504 cals)	Spicy Beef Tacos, p. 162 (371 cals)	One-tray Roast Chook & Veg, p. 136 (539 cals) (Eat 1, keep 1, freeze 2)
Ridiculous Roast Veg, p. 108 (275 cals) (Eat 1, keep 1, freeze 2)	Cajun Cauliflower Clusters, p. 102 (477 cals)	Cajun Cauliflower Clusters, p. 102 (477 cals) (Leftovers)	Sweet Potato Nuggets, p. 96 (398 cals)

THURSDAY	FRIDAY	SATURDAY	SUNDAY
One-bowl Banana Bread, p. 170 (347 cals) (Leftovers)	Black Forest Brownie, p. 179 (263 cals)	Bangin' Bounty-licious Bar, p. 182 (290 cals)	One-bowl Banana Bread, p. 170 (347 cals) (Leftovers)
Choc Peanut Butter Cookie, p. 173 (200 cals)	Carrot Cake Muffin, p. 185 (291 cals)	No-bake Banoffee Slice, p. 176 (317 cals)	Choc Peanut Butter Cookie, p. 173 (200 cals)

FIVE IN FIVE

MEAL PLAN 3

	MONDAY	TUESDAY	WEDNESDAY
BREAKFAST	Overnight Protein Oats, p. 76 (453 cals)	Banana Berry Protein Muffins, p. 79 (392 cals) (Eat 1, keep 2, freeze 3)	Golden Granola Clusters, p. 74 (472 cals)
LUNCH	One-tray Roast Chook & Veg, p. 136 (539 cals) (Leftovers)	Chicken Pesto Pasta, p. 145 (671 cals)	Chicken Pesto Pasta, p. 145 (671 cals) (Leftovers)
DINNER	Bangkok Barramundi in a Bag, p. 126 (325 cals)	Middle Eastern Turkey Burger, p. 153 (443 cals)	Crispy Skin Salmon with Broccoli & Pea Puree, p. 131 (416 cals)
SIDE	Sweet Potato Nuggets, p. 96 (398 cals)	Salty Charred Greens, p. 112 (196 cals)	Salty Charred Greens, p. 112 (196 cals) (Leftovers)
SNACK #1	One-bowl Banana Bread, p. 170 (347 cals)	Black Forest Brownie, p. 179 (263 cals)	Bangin' Bounty-licious Bar, p. 182 (290 cals)
SNACK #2	Choc Peanut Butter Cookie, p. 173 (200 cals)	Carrot Cake Muffin, p. 185 (291 cals)	No-bake Banoffee Slice, p. 176 (317 cals)

MEAL PLAN

3

THURSDAY	FRIDAY	SATURDAY	SUNDAY
Banana Berry Protein Muffins, p. 79 (392 cals) (Leftovers)	Golden Granola Clusters, p. 74 (472 cals) (Leftovers)	Banana Berry Protein Muffins, p. 79 (392 cals) (Leftovers)	The Scandi, p. 80 (479 cals)
Phuket Pork & Pineapple Salad, p. 154 (400 cals)	Phuket Pork & Pineapple Salad, p. 154 (400 cals) (Leftovers)	Speedy Chicken Souva, p. 148 (446 cals) (Leftovers)	Brilliant Beef Rendang, p. 165 (499 cals) (Leftovers)
Classic Steak Frites, p. 159 (493 cals)	Speedy Chicken Souva, p. 148 (446 cals)	Brilliant Beef Rendang, p. 165 (499 cals)	Spicy Beef Tacos, p. 162 (371 cals)
Cajun Cauliflower Clusters p. 102 (477 cals)	Cajun Cauliflower Clusters, p. 102 (477 cals) (Leftovers)	Gorgeous Green Curry, p. 105 (442 cals)	Next-level Nacho Bowl, p. 99 (392 cals)

One-bowl Banana Bread, p. 170 (347 cals) (Leftovers)	Black Forest Brownie, p. 179 (263 cals)	Bangin' Bounty-licious Bar, p. 182 (290 cals)	One-bowl Banana Bread, p. 170 (347 cals) (Leftovers)
Choc Peanut Butter Cookie, p. 173 (200 cals)	Carrot Cake Muffin, p. 185 (291 cals)	No-bake Banoffee Slice, p. 176 (317 cals)	Choc Peanut Butter Cookie, p. 173 (200 cals)

FIVE IN FIVE

MEAL PLAN 4

	MONDAY	TUESDAY	WEDNESDAY
BREAKFAST	Golden Granola Clusters, p. 74 (472 cals) (Leftovers) + Banana Split Thickshake, p. 63 (248 cals)	Phenomenal Frittata, p. 86 (297 cals) (Leftovers) + Perfect Popeye, p. 64 (252 cals)	Golden Granola Clusters, p. 74 (472 cals) (Leftovers)
LUNCH	Spicy Beef Tacos, p. 162 (371 cals) (Leftovers)	Thai-style Fish Cakes, p. 122 (346 cals) (Leftovers)	Sensational Satay Skewers, p. 156 (536 cals) (Leftovers)
DINNER	Thai-style Fish Cakes, p. 122 (346 cals)	Sensational Satay Skewers, p. 156 (536 cals)	Bangkok Barramundi in a Bag, p. 126 (325 cals)
SIDE	Phenomenal Frittata, p. 86 (297 cals) (Eat 1, keep 1, freeze 2)	Crispy Mexican Corn Ribs, p. 111 (384 cals)	Crispy Mexican Corn Ribs, p. 111 (384 cals) (Leftovers)

SNACK #1	One-bowl Banana Bread, p. 170 (347 cals)	Black Forest Brownie, p. 179 (263 cals)	Bangin' Bounty-licious Bar, p. 182 (290 cals)
SNACK #2	Choc Peanut Butter Cookie, p. 173 (200 cals)	Carrot Cake Muffin, p. 185 (291 cals)	No-bake Banoffee Slice, p. 176 (317 cals)

MEAL PLAN

4

THURSDAY	FRIDAY	SATURDAY	SUNDAY
Choc Protein Coffee Crusher, p. 62 (258 cals)	Caramelised Banana & Cinnamon Porridge, p. 70 (356 cals)	Garlicky Hash Browns, p. 88 (586 cals)	Sticky Strawberry Protein Pancakes, p. 73 (572 cals)
Smashed Salmon Salad, p. 116 (555 cals)	Smashed Salmon Salad, p. 116 (555 cals) (Leftovers)	Chicken Pesto Pasta, p. 145 (671 cals) (Leftovers)	Garlicky Hash Browns, p. 88 (586 cals) (Leftovers)
Chicken Pesto Pasta, p. 145 (671 cals)	Chicken Satay Burger, p. 142 (558 cals)	Salmon Zaghetti, p. 119 (258 cals)	Butter Chicken Bow, p. 134 (388 cals) (Eat 1, keep 1, freeze 2)
Spicy Stuffed Mushrooms, p. 100 (260 cals)	Spicy Stuffed Mushrooms, p. 100 (260 cals) (Leftovers)	Salty Charred Greens, p. 112 (196 cals)	Salty Charred Greens, p. 112 (196 cals) (Leftovers)

One-bowl Banana Bread, p. 170 (347 cals) (Leftovers)	Black Forest Brownie, p. 179 (263 cals)	Bangin' Bounty-licious Bar, p. 182 (290 cals)	One-bowl Banana Bread, p. 170 (347 cals) (Leftovers)
Choc Peanut Butter Cookie, p. 173 (200 cals)	Carrot Cake Muffin, p. 185 (291 cals)	No-bake Banoffee Slice, p. 176 (317 cals)	Choc Peanut Butter Cookie, p. 173 (200 cals)

FIVE IN FIVE

MEAL PLAN 5

	MONDAY	TUESDAY	WEDNESDAY
BREAKFAST	Golden Granola Clusters, p. 74 (472 cals) + Peanut Butter Bullet Train, p. 63 (228 cals)	Banana Berry Protein Muffin, p. 79 (392 cals) (Eat 1, keep 1, freeze 4) + Black Forest Bliss, p. 67 (261 cals)	Golden Granola Clusters, p. 74 (472 cals) (Leftovers)
LUNCH	Salmon Zaghetti, p. 119 (258 cals)	Next-level Nacho Bowl, p. 99 (392 cals)	One-tray Roast Chook & Veg, p. 136 (539 cals) (Leftovers)
DINNER	Butter Chicken Bow, p. 134 (388 cals) (Leftovers)	One-tray Roast Chook & Veg, p. 136 (539 cals) (Eat 1, keep 1, freeze 2)	Crispy Skin Salmon with Broccoli & Pea Puree, p. 131 (416 cals)
SIDE	Gorgeous Green Curry, p. 105 (442 cals)	Chilli Charred Cabbage, p. 94 (185 cals)	Phenomenal Frittata, p. 86 (297 cals) (Eat 1, keep 1, freeze 2)
SNACK #1	No-bake Banoffee Slice, p. 176 (317 cals)	Black Forest Brownie, p. 179 (263 cals)	Bangin' Bounty-licious Bar, p. 182 (290 cals)
SNACK #2	Choc Peanut Butter Cookie, p. 173 (200 cals)	Carrot Cake Muffin, p. 185 (291 cals)	No-bake Banoffee Slice, p. 176 (317 cals)

MEAL PLAN

5

THURSDAY	FRIDAY	SATURDAY	SUNDAY
Banana Berry Protein Muffin, p. 79 (392 cals) (Leftovers) + Perfect Popeye, p. 64 (252 cals)	Golden Granola Clusters, p. 74 (472 cals) (Leftovers)	The Scandi, p. 80 (479 cals)	Golden Granola Clusters, p. 74 (472 cals) (Leftovers)
Phenomenal Frittata, p. 86 (297 cals) (Leftovers)	Chicken Pesto Pasta, p. 145 (671 cals) (Leftovers)	Thai-style Fish Cakes, p. 122 (346 cals) (Leftovers)	Lukey's Lamb Pizza, p. 166 (609 cals) (Leftovers)
Chicken Pesto Pasta, p. 145 (671 cals)	Thai-style Fish Cakes, p. 122 (346 cals) (Eat 1, keep 1, freeze 2)	Lukey's Lamb Pizza, p. 166 (609 cals)	Middle Eastern Turkey Burger, p. 153 (443 cals)
Chilli Charred Cabbage, p. 94 (185 cals) (Leftovers)	Crispy Pumpkin Salad, p. 93 (261 cals)	Crispy Pumpkin Salad, p. 93 (261 cals) (Leftovers)	Charred Salty Greens, p. 112 (196 cals)

No-bake Banoffee Slice, p. 176 (317 cals)	Black Forest Brownie, p. 179 (263 cals)	Bangin' Bounty-licious Bar, p. 182 (290 cals)	Carrot Cake Muffin, p. 185 (291 cals)
Choc Peanut Butter Cookie, p. 173 (200 cals)	Carrot Cake Muffin, p. 185 (291 cals)	No-bake Banoffee Slice, p. 176 (317 cals)	Choc Peanut Butter Cookie, p. 173 (200 cals)

FIVE IN FIVE

DRI

NKS

PINEAPPLE COLADA SMOOTHIE

Transport yourself to a tropical island anywhere, anytime, with this high-protein summer smoothie.

75 g (½ cup) diced frozen pineapple, plus extra to serve
½ frozen banana (60 g), diced
125 ml (½ cup) coconut water
40 g scoop vanilla plant-based protein powder
2 teaspoons (7 g) toasted shredded coconut

SERVES 1

Place all the ingredients except the shredded coconut in a food processor or high-speed blender and blitz until well combined. Pour into a glass and serve topped with the extra pineapple and the shredded coconut.

NEXT LEVEL IT: For a thicker, creamier smoothie and some extra calories and healthy fats, you can add 3 tablespoons of canned coconut cream.

PRO TIP: Pineapple contains a powerful digestive enzyme called bromelain, which helps break down nutrients in our gut for optimal absorption, making sure you get the most out of what you eat.

DF GF PB RSF

THE STATS PER SERVE

Cals: 306 | Protein: 29.7 g | Fat: 6.7 g | Carbs: 29.6 g

CHOC PROTEIN COFFEE CRUSHER

Coffee and chocolate are the ultimate companions: here, the richness of the cacao powder really goes well with the bold coffee flavour, and the maple syrup cuts through both beautifully.

250 ml (1 cup) strong brewed coffee or double shot long black, chilled
40 g scoop chocolate protein powder (see Pro Tip)
1 teaspoon cacao powder
1 tablespoon maple syrup (optional)

5 IN 5 PANTRY STAPLES

135 g (1 cup) ice cubes

SERVES 1

Place all the ingredients in a food processor or high-speed blender and whiz until just combined. You don't want the ice to break up completely, you want a frappé-like consistency. Pour into a tall glass and sprinkle with some extra cacao powder.

NEXT LEVEL IT: Add a dash of your favourite milk for a creamier texture and garnish with raw cacao nibs if you've got some.

PRO TIP: Protein powders vary from brand to brand, so whether you use plant based, collagen or whey based make sure a 40 g scoop contains 30 g protein, is naturally sweetened with stevia or monk fruit, and is low carb, without any added nasties.

DF GF PB RSF

THE STATS PER SERVE

Cals: 258 | Protein: 30.6 g | Fat: 3.9 g | Carbs: 23.4 g

BANANA SPLIT THICKSHAKE

Stay on track with your goals and treat yourself to the flavours of a banana split without the excess calories. You'll never feel like you're missing out again.

1 frozen banana (120 g), chopped into small pieces
125 ml (½ cup) unsweetened almond or coconut milk
2 strawberries, cut into wedges
1 teaspoon cacao nibs
1 teaspoon toasted peanuts, roughly chopped

SERVES 1

Combine the banana and almond or coconut milk in a food processor. Blitz until thick and creamy – add a splash or two of water, if needed, to get it moving. Pour into a tall glass and top with the strawberry wedges, cacao nibs and peanuts.

NEXT LEVEL IT: If you want this as a pre- or post-workout smoothie, you can always add a scoop of your favourite protein powder. Add enough to give yourself 30 g of quality protein.

PRO TIP: The calories in different types of milk vary depending on whether they are sweetened, unsweetened, high or low in fat, or contain other additives. Always read the labels so you know exactly what you're getting.

DF GF PB RSF

THE STATS PER SERVE

Cals: 248 | Protein: 4.4 g | Fat: 8.9 g | Carbs: 41.1 g

PEANUT BUTTER BULLET TRAIN

And by 'train', I mean gain train, an energy and muscle gain train. Coffee paired with healthy fats and collagen is the ultimate way to kickstart your day for energy, focus and repair.

250 ml (1 cup) strong brewed coffee or double shot long black
30 g scoop vanilla collagen powder
2 teaspoons smooth peanut butter
1 teaspoon MCT oil
½ teaspoon ground cinnamon, to serve

SERVES 1

Combine the coffee, collagen powder, peanut butter and MCT oil in a heat-safe blender and blitz on low until smooth and creamy (the peanut butter will break down completely and emulsify and thicken). Pour into a large mug, sprinkle with the cinnamon and enjoy immediately.

NEXT LEVEL IT: Depending on the sweetness of the vanilla collagen powder you use, you may like to add a dash of your favourite sweetener, such as maple syrup, honey or monk fruit.

PRO TIP: When choosing a vanilla collagen powder, look for one that's naturally vanilla flavoured, low carb and sweetened with stevia or monk fruit to avoid any processed or refined sugars.

DF GF LC RSF

THE STATS PER SERVE

Cals: 228 | Protein: 23.8 g | Fat: 10.7 g | Carbs: 7.9 g

PERFECT POPEYE

YOU WILL NEED

½ frozen banana (60 g), chopped into small pieces
½ green apple (50 g), cored and diced
2 cubes frozen spinach (see Pro Tip)
125 ml (½ cup) coconut water
30 g scoop vanilla protein powder or unflavoured collagen powder

5 IN 5 PANTRY STAPLES

70 g (½ cup) ice cubes

SERVES 1

THE STATS PER SERVE

Cals: 252
Protein: 23.1 g
Fat: 1.0 g
Carbs: 36.8 g

DF GF RSF

Place all the ingredients in a food processor or high-speed blender and blitz until well combined and your desired consistency. For a chunkier smoothie, don't blitz too long; for a smoother consistency, blitz on high for longer. Pour into a glass and enjoy.

NEXT LEVEL IT: Green vegetables are low in calories and high in essential nutrients, meaning that you can always up your green goodness by adding extra to this recipe. Sliced cucumber, kale leaves or even a powdered green supplement work wonderfully in this smoothie.

PRO TIP: I recommend frozen spinach for this recipe because it's really cheap to buy in bulk, is equally as nutritious as its fresh counterpart and is much easier to add to smoothies like this.

Popeye was famous for getting his big muscles from eating all that spinach. This recipe can help with your muscle gains, but with a whole lot more flavour than boring raw spinach.

This protein-packed smoothie is the ultimate black forest flavour combination, pairing chocolate with dark forest fruits. The result is a thick and creamy pre- or post-workout smoothie, or high-protein snack for any time of day.

BLACK FOREST BLISS

YOU WILL NEED

70 g (½ cup) mixed frozen berries, dark fruit blend if possible (blackberries, cherries, blackcurrants), plus 1 tablespoon extra to serve
125 ml (½ cup) coconut water
40 g scoop chocolate plant-based protein powder
1 teaspoon cacao nibs, plus a few extra to serve

5 IN 5 PANTRY STAPLES

70 g (½ cup) ice cubes

SERVES 1

THE STATS PER SERVE

Cals: 261
Protein: 29.5 g
Fat: 5.6 g
Carbs: 18.9 g

DF GF PB RSF

Combine all the ingredients in a food processor or high-speed blender and blitz until smooth, thick and well combined. Pour into a glass and serve with the extra berries and cacao nibs. Enjoy immediately.

NEXT LEVEL IT: Lightly toasted shredded coconut works a treat in this recipe, so if you're looking for extra calories and to up your healthy fats, look no further than a generous sprinkle on top.

PRO TIP: Frozen fruit and berries are an economical way to enjoy produce that isn't in season. The nutrition is locked in and you minimise wastage by using only what you need.

FIVE IN FIVE

BREA

KFAST

CARAMELISED BANANA & CINNAMON PORRIDGE

YOU WILL NEED

45 g (½ cup) gluten-free rolled oats (see page 30)
½ teaspoon ground cinnamon, plus a little extra for sprinkling
1 tablespoon fine coconut sugar, plus a little extra for sprinkling
1 banana (about 120 g), sliced diagonally
2 tablespoons plain Greek yoghurt or coconut yoghurt

5 IN 5 PANTRY STAPLES

250 ml (1 cup) filtered water
1 teaspoon coconut oil

SERVES 1

THE STATS PER SERVE

Cals: 356
Protein: 10.1 g
Fat: 8.8 g
Carbs: 59.4 g

Combine the oats, cinnamon and filtered water in a saucepan, place over low heat and cook, stirring occasionally, for 6–8 minutes, or until the oats have softened and the porridge is thick and creamy.

Meanwhile, place the coconut oil, coconut sugar and a splash of water in a small frying pan over medium heat and stir until the sugar has melted. Add the sliced banana and fry on each side for 3–4 minutes, or until golden, softened and caramelised.

Spoon the porridge into a bowl, top with the caramelised banana, dollop on your yoghurt of choice and sprinkle with the extra cinnamon and coconut sugar, if you like.

NEXT LEVEL IT: If you're looking to up your daily protein, simply add a scoop of your favourite protein powder and an extra 125 ml (½ cup) of water to your porridge.

PRO TIP: To make this dish more nutritious, simply include a small handful of walnuts for healthy fats, cacao nibs for magnesium and crunch, and berries for antioxidants.

DF* GF* PB RSF

Some people relegate porridge to the winter months, but I am an advocate for celebrating this high-protein soul-warming dish all year round, as it is just too delicious.

I love pancakes, especially the kind I know are good for me – like these ones that are loaded with quality protein and healthy fats. This is *the* most delicious way to enjoy strawberries.

STICKY STRAWBERRY PROTEIN PANCAKES

YOU WILL NEED

1 very ripe banana (about 120 g)
3 eggs, whisked
20 g scoop vanilla plant-based protein powder
2 teaspoons maple syrup
70 g (½ cup) sliced strawberries

5 IN 5 PANTRY STAPLES

1 tablespoon tapioca flour
2 teaspoons extra-virgin olive oil

SERVES 1

THE STATS PER SERVE

Cals: 572
Protein: 34.8 g
Fat: 26.5 g
Carbs: 50.2 g

DF GF RSF

Place the banana in a large bowl and mash with the back of a fork or a whisk. Whisk in the eggs to incorporate, then add the protein powder and tapioca flour and whisk well.

Heat 1 teaspoon of the olive oil in a large, non-stick frying pan over medium–high heat. Working in batches, add ¼ cup of batter per pancake to the pan, allowing enough room between each one for flipping, and cook for 3–4 minutes on each side until golden brown. You will get four pancakes.

Meanwhile, heat the remaining olive oil in a small frying pan over medium heat, add the maple syrup and strawberries and sauté for 5–6 minutes, or until the strawberries are softened and caramelised around the edges.

Serve your pancakes topped with the lovely sticky strawberries.

NEXT LEVEL IT: Add a dollop of your favourite high-protein yoghurt to up the protein, some toasted coconut flakes to increase the healthy fats, or a drizzle of maple syrup for some extra carbs post training.

PRO TIP: Some people worry that heating protein denatures its nutrient value, but most protein powders can withstand temperatures of up to 160°C before any damage is done.

GOLDEN GRANOLA CLUSTERS

YOU WILL NEED

180 g (2 cups) gluten-free rolled oats (see page 30)
175 g (½ cup) honey or maple syrup
3 tablespoons dried blueberries
1 teaspoon ground cinnamon
500 g (2 cups) plain Greek yoghurt or high-protein yoghurt of choice or dairy-free alternative

5 IN 5 PANTRY STAPLES

2 tablespoons coconut oil
sea salt

SERVES 4

THE STATS PER SERVE

Cals: 472
Protein: 19.2 g
Fat: 12.8 g
Carbs: 66.7 g

DF* GF* PB RSF

Preheat the oven to 160°C and line a large baking tray with baking paper.

Combine the oats, honey or maple syrup, dried blueberries, cinnamon, coconut oil and a pinch of salt in a large bowl.

Spread the mixture over the tray in a thin layer. Bake for 20–25 minutes until golden brown, gently stirring after 15 minutes, being careful not to break the mixture into small pieces. Set aside and allow to cool completely and crisp up.

To serve, break into chunky clusters and enjoy with a dollop of yoghurt – 125 g (½ cup) per serve – or grab as a snack on the go. Store leftovers in an airtight container for up to 7 days.

NEXT LEVEL IT: If you want to get creative, for added nutrition and texture, you can add nuts, seeds and other dried fruit to the base granola mixture before the clusters hit the oven. Some fresh blueberries to serve are lovely too.

PRO TIP: Looking to increase your protein with this meal? Mix a scoop of your favourite protein powder into a small amount of your favourite milk and pour over the top as you would with any other cereal.

I love mueslis and granola – they're really simple to make, plus you can mix and match your flavour combinations. Start with this as your base and follow my hints and tips to take yours to the next level.

OVERNIGHT PROTEIN OATS

YOU WILL NEED

45 g (½ cup) gluten-free rolled oats (see page 30)
40 g scoop vanilla plant-based protein powder
250 ml (1 cup) coconut water
125 g (1 cup) frozen mixed berries, plus extra to serve
2 tablespoons low-fat high-protein plain Greek yoghurt or coconut yoghurt, to serve

SERVES 1

THE STATS PER SERVE

Cals: 453
Protein: 38 g
Fat: 6.5 g
Carbs: 52 g

DF* GF* PB RSF

Combine the oats, protein powder, coconut water and berries in a large jar or bowl and mix well. For a more paste-like bircher muesli consistency, use less liquid; for a runnier consistency, add more coconut water or water.

Cover the oat mixture and transfer to the fridge overnight so the oats absorb all the liquid and the berries thaw.

The next day, enjoy your overnight oats topped with the yoghurt and extra berries.

NEXT LEVEL IT: I love adding a grated green apple to the oat mixture before it goes into the fridge overnight; it's a great way to up the flavour and fibre content.

PRO TIP: For extra carbs, add some dried fruit; for increased healthy fats, add some nuts and seeds; and for extra protein and fibre, add some chia seeds.

Overnight oats have got to be one of the quickest ways to make sure you hit your nutrition goals each and every day. Preparing your oats in bulk, ahead of time, ensures you always have something epic to start your day.

People often consider muffins a 'sometimes' treat-type food, but when they are as nutritious and delicious as these, they are something you can enjoy for breakfast, a snack, or just because. They're that good.

BANANA BERRY PROTEIN MUFFINS

YOU WILL NEED

3 ripe bananas (about 360 g), 2 mashed, 1 sliced into 6 discs
4 large eggs
125 ml (½ cup) maple syrup
180 g (1 cup) vanilla plant-based protein powder
135 g (1 heaped cup) frozen mixed berries

5 IN 5 PANTRY STAPLES

3 tablespoons melted coconut oil
3 tablespoons tapioca flour
2 teaspoons gluten-free baking powder
½ teaspoon sea salt

MAKES 6

THE STATS PER SERVE

Cals: 392
Protein: 26.2 g
Fat: 13.3 g
Carbs: 40.6 g

Preheat the oven to 180°C and line a large six-hole muffin tin with paper cases.

Place the mashed banana in a large bowl, add the eggs and use a whisk to continue to mash and combine well. Add the maple syrup and coconut oil and mix with a spoon until incorporated. Add the protein powder, tapioca flour, baking powder and salt and mix well to form a thick, chunky batter. Carefully fold in most of the mixed berries, reserving a small handful for the topping.

Pour the muffin batter evenly into the tin, then gently press the reserved berries and a banana disc on top of each muffin. Bake for 20–30 minutes, or until the muffins haven risen, are golden brown on top and a toothpick inserted in the centre comes out mostly clean. Allow the muffins to cool in the tin for 10 minutes or so before carefully removing.

One muffin is one serve, so eat one fresh out of the oven. Store the remaining muffins in an airtight container in the fridge to enjoy for up to 5 days or freeze for up to 3 months.

NEXT LEVEL IT: To mix up the flavour combinations, switch the protein powder flavour you use. Chocolate makes these ridiculously moreish.

PRO TIP: If you don't have a muffin tin, this mixture works wonderfully well as a high-protein loaf. Simply bake in a small loaf tin for 30–40 minutes.

DF GF RSF

THE SCANDI

YOU WILL NEED

2 eggs
¼ avocado, sliced into wedges
½ Lebanese cucumber, sliced into thin wedges diagonally
80 g smoked salmon slices
1 small handful of dill sprigs

5 IN 5 PANTRY STAPLES

2 teaspoons extra-virgin olive oil
2 teaspoons lemon juice
sea salt and freshly ground black pepper

SERVES 1

THE STATS PER SERVE

Cals: 479
Protein: 33.4 g
Fat: 35.6 g
Carbs: 7.8 g

DF GF LC RSF

Place the eggs in a small saucepan, fill with cold water to come 2.5 cm above the eggs and bring to the boil over high heat. Once boiling, remove from the heat and cover with the lid. Set aside and allow the eggs to cook to your liking – 4 minutes for soft boiled, 6 minutes for medium and 8 minutes for hard boiled. Transfer the eggs to a bowl of cold water and allow to cool for 10 minutes before peeling and halving.

Meanwhile, to make a dressing, whisk together the olive oil, lemon juice and a generous pinch of salt and pepper in a small jug.

To serve, plate up the avocado and cucumber, fold the smoked salmon into curls and arrange alongside. Add the halved eggs, pour the dressing over the top and scatter with the dill.

NEXT LEVEL IT: If you're looking for carbohydrates to pair with this recipe, look no further than the Scandinavian classic of finely sliced and toasted rye bread. If you're gluten free, any gluten-free alternative will work well too.

PRO TIP: Leftover ham on the bone is a great substitute for the salmon, especially around Christmas time.

Nordic countries celebrate certain key staples in their meals, and a Scandi breakfast wouldn't be complete without boiled eggs, a dairy or fat of some sort, cured meat and some veg. Inspired by these key elements, I've created a spectacular breakfast that's also incredibly easy to make.

SWEET POTATO OMELETTE

YOU WILL NEED

2–3 small sweet potatoes, (400 g) scrubbed
½ red onion, finely sliced
6 eggs
10 mixed cherry tomatoes, quartered or sliced
1 tablespoon roughly chopped coriander leaves

5 IN 5 PANTRY STAPLES

1 tablespoon extra-virgin olive oil
sea salt and freshly ground black pepper
½ teaspoon chilli flakes

SERVES 2

THE STATS PER SERVE

Cals: 440
Protein: 21.9 g
Fat: 24.9 g
Carbs: 33.3 g

DF GF RSF

Bring a saucepan of salted water to the boil, add the sweet potatoes and cook for 8–10 minutes, or until they are soft when pierced with a fork; you don't want them to be mushy. Remove from the heat and allow them to cool slightly, then peel and carefully slice the flesh lengthways into long 5 mm thick pieces.

Heat one-third of the olive oil in a non-stick frying pan over medium–high heat. Add the onion and sauté for 3–4 minutes, or until softened and lightly caramelised. Remove the pan from the heat, transfer the onion to a plate and set aside.

Add another one-third of the olive oil to the same pan, then carefully layer in one-third of the sweet potato, overlapping the pieces slightly to create a base for your omelette. Spread half the onion over the sweet potato layer. Repeat with another one-third of the sweet potato and all the onion and finish with a layer of the remaining sweet potato.

Whisk the eggs with a pinch of salt and pepper in a bowl, then pour the egg over the sweet potato, making sure the eggy goodness seeps into the gaps and you get all-over coverage.

To make a spicy tomato salsa, combine the cherry tomatoes and coriander with the remaining olive oil, the chilli flakes and a generous pinch of salt and pepper in a bowl and mix well.

Preheat the oven grill.

Place the pan over medium–low heat, cover with a lid and cook for 10–12 minutes, or until the egg begins to set.

Transfer the pan to the oven and grill for 6–8 minutes, or until the omelette is cooked through.

To serve, carefully place a clean plate on top of the pan and flip the omelette onto the plate. Slice the omelette into wedges and top with the spicy tomato salsa. Store leftovers in an airtight container in the fridge and enjoy cold for lunch the next day.

NEXT LEVEL IT: A generous squeeze of lemon or lime juice works wonderfully with the salsa.

PRO TIP: Swap the sweet potato for a waxy potato variety – such as coliban or desiree – or butternut pumpkin, if you like.

A traditional Spanish omelette, also known as tortilla de patatas, is a simple combination of eggs, potato and onion. I've used this base as inspiration and added some personal touches.

You know I love a fritter, and here I share the ultimate way to make sure they're crispy every time. What could be a more perfect start to the day?

CRISPY PUMPKIN FRITTERS

YOU WILL NEED

400 g butternut pumpkin, peeled and cut into 3 cm pieces
5 eggs
1 garlic clove, crushed
½ avocado, finely diced
10 cherry tomatoes, quartered or finely diced

5 IN 5 PANTRY STAPLES

3 tablespoons tapioca flour
1 tablespoon dried parsley
sea salt and freshly ground black pepper
125 ml (½ cup) extra-virgin olive oil, plus 1 tablespoon extra
¼ teaspoon chilli flakes

SERVES 2

THE STATS PER SERVE

Cals: 502
Protein: 19.5 g
Fat: 34.2 g
Carbs: 35.3 g

DF GF RSF

To get started on your fritters, steam the pumpkin until very soft. Mash and set aside to cool slightly.

Combine 1 egg with the tapioca flour, garlic, dried parsley and a pinch of salt in a large bowl and whisk well. Add the mashed pumpkin and mix to form a thick batter.

Heat 125 ml (½ cup) of the olive oil in a large deep frying pan over medium–high heat until it reaches 180°C or a small piece of pumpkin batter sizzles when added. Working in batches if needed, add heaped tablespoon amounts of the batter to the hot oil and fry for 3–4 minutes on each side, or until golden brown on all sides. Transfer to paper towel to drain. You should get 16 fritters.

Meanwhile, fry the remaining eggs in the extra 1 tablespoon of olive oil in a large non-stick frying pan over medium–high heat, sunny side up, until just cooked.

To make an avocado salsa, combine the avocado, tomato and chilli flakes with a pinch of salt and pepper in a small bowl and gently mix (without mashing the avo).

To serve, plate up the eggs with the pumpkin fritters, then add generous dollops of the avocado salsa, season well and eat. Store leftovers in an airtight container in the fridge and enjoy cold for lunch the next day.

NEXT LEVEL IT: Citrus cuts through the richness of the avocado wonderfully, so feel free to add a squeeze of lemon or lime juice to your salsa.

PRO TIP: You can reduce the calories in this dish by using an air fryer. Prepare your fritters, spray them lightly with olive oil and air fry until golden brown, crispy and cooked through.

PHENOMENAL FRITTATA

YOU WILL NEED

600 g butternut pumpkin, skin on and cut into 2 cm cubes
1 small red onion (about 125 g), finely sliced
12 cherry tomatoes (about 180 g), halved
100 g (2¼ cups) baby spinach leaves
8 eggs

5 IN 5 PANTRY STAPLES

2 tablespoons extra-virgin olive oil
sea salt and freshly ground black pepper
½ teaspoon chilli flakes

SERVES 4

THE STATS PER SERVE

Cals: 297
Protein: 15.7 g
Fat: 19.9 g
Carbs: 17.9 g

DF GF LC RSF

Preheat the oven to 180°C and line a baking tray with baking paper.

Place the pumpkin on the tray, drizzle with 1 tablespoon of the olive oil, season well with salt and toss to coat. Roast for 15–20 minutes, or until softened and beginning to caramelise and go golden brown around the edges.

Meanwhile, heat the remaining olive oil in a large, ovenproof, non-stick frying pan over medium heat. Add the onion and sauté for 3–4 minutes, or until softened and beginning to go golden brown. Stir in the cherry tomatoes and cook for 2 minutes, or until slightly softened, then add the baby spinach and stir for 30–60 seconds, or until just starting to wilt. Remove from the heat, add the roast pumpkin and set aside.

Whisk the eggs, chilli flakes and a generous pinch of salt and pepper in a large bowl. Pour the egg mixture over the roast pumpkin mixture in the pan and gently mix to evenly distribute. Cook, moving the mixture around the pan, until the egg starts to set around the edges. Transfer the pan to the oven and bake for 12–15 minutes, or until the eggs are cooked through and the frittata is golden brown on top. Finish under the oven grill if necessary.

Set the frittata aside to cool slightly before dividing into four even portions. Season well with salt and pepper and serve. Store the leftovers in an airtight container in the fridge for up to 3 days.

NEXT LEVEL IT: This recipe is incredibly versatile so experiment with different flavour combinations and add whatever vegetables, herbs and spices you've got on hand.

PRO TIP: If you're looking to up the carbs, you can swap the pumpkin for coliban or desiree potatoes or sweet potato.

Frittata is such a delicious and easy way to pack loads of vegetables into your breakfast. Plus, it's the perfect recipe to make in bulk so you have a nutritious meal to enjoy hot or cold at any time of day throughout the week.

GARLICKY HASH BROWNS

YOU WILL NEED

280 g (2 cups) grated potato (desiree or coliban work well)
2 garlic cloves, crushed
½ teaspoon onion powder
5 eggs
60 g smoked salmon slices

5 IN 5 PANTRY STAPLES

3 tablespoons tapioca flour
sea salt and freshly ground black pepper
2 tablespoons extra-virgin olive oil
¼ teaspoon chilli flakes (optional)

SERVES 2

THE STATS PER SERVE

Cals: 586
Protein: 25.7 g
Fat: 34.6 g
Carbs: 43.7 g

DF GF RSF

Rinse the grated potato in a fine sieve until the water runs clear, then squeeze out all the excess liquid by wrapping the potato in a clean tea towel and twisting. You want the grated potato to be as dry as possible – this process will make your hash browns crispier than ever.

Combine the potato, garlic, onion powder, tapioca flour, 1 teaspoon of salt and 1 egg in a large bowl and mix with a fork until well incorporated.

Heat 1 tablespoon of the olive oil in a large frying pan over medium–high heat, then add heaped tablespoon amounts of the hash brown batter to the pan, using about half the mixture. Cook for 5–6 minutes, or until golden brown around the edges and beginning to cook through, then flip and continue to cook for another 5–6 minutes, or until golden brown, crispy and completely cooked through. Transfer to a plate and keep warm in a low oven. Repeat this process with the remaining oil and batter to make six hash browns.

Meanwhile, bring a saucepan of water to the boil, crack in the remaining eggs and poach to your liking. Carefully remove them with a slotted spoon and set aside ready for serving.

To plate up, make your hash browns the base, add a layer of smoked salmon and then top with your perfectly poached eggs. Season well with salt and pepper and scatter with the chilli flakes, if using. Store leftovers in an airtight container in the fridge and enjoy for lunch or dinner the next day.

NEXT LEVEL IT: Sprigs of dill or flat-leaf parsley work a treat sprinkled on top of the finished dish.

PRO TIP: For a slightly sweeter flavour, swap out the potato for sweet potato; or for a lower carb option, use butternut pumpkin.

I love all things golden brown, crispy and crunchy, which is why I think I gravitate towards recipes for fritters and hash browns. This is a classic combo – straight up potato hash with the goodness of smoked salmon on top. Enjoy!

FIVE IN FIVE

SAL
VEG &

ADS,
SIDES

Salads can sometimes seem boring so, to take them to the next level, I love adding different textures – like making the pumpkin I use extra crispy, as I do here.

CRISPY PUMPKIN SALAD

YOU WILL NEED

400 g kent pumpkin, skin on, deseeded and cut into thin wedges
1 tablespoon pistachio dukkah, plus a little extra to serve
180 g (4 cups) mixed salad leaves
125 g (½ cup) plain Greek yoghurt or dairy-free alternative
2 teaspoons maple syrup

5 IN 5 PANTRY STAPLES

2 tablespoons extra-virgin olive oil
1 tablespoon tapioca flour
juice of 1 lemon or lime
¼ teaspoon chilli flakes
sea salt and freshly ground black pepper

SERVES 2

THE STATS PER SERVE

Cals: 261
Protein: 3.6 g
Fat: 12.8 g
Carbs: 29.4 g

DF* GF PB RSF

Preheat the oven to 200°C and line a baking tray with baking paper.

Place the pumpkin in a large bowl, drizzle with 1 tablespoon of the olive oil, add the tapioca flour and dukkah and mix with your hands to coat well (this will give the pumpkin a lovely crispy crust on the outside). Arrange the pumpkin in a single layer on the tray and roast for 20–25 minutes, turning after 10 minutes, until golden brown and cooked all the way through. Set aside to cool slightly.

Meanwhile, place the salad leaves in a large bowl and drizzle with the remaining olive oil and the lemon or lime juice, then gently toss.

To make a dressing, whisk together the yoghurt, maple syrup and chilli flakes in a small bowl.

To serve, scatter the dressed salad leaves on a plate, top with the crispy warm pumpkin wedges, drizzle with the maple yoghurt dressing and finish with a sprinkle of extra dukkah and a pinch of salt and pepper. Store leftovers in an airtight container in the fridge and enjoy for lunch the next day.

NEXT LEVEL IT: To increase the vitamins, minerals and healthy fats in this salad, include some avocado – it also adds great flavour and texture.

PRO TIP: Fibre is a huge component in weight loss, which is why I say keep the pumpkin skin on, as it's loaded with the stuff.

CHILLI CHARRED CABBAGE

YOU WILL NEED

1 garlic clove, crushed
1 tablespoon wholegrain mustard
1 tablespoon maple syrup
2 tablespoons finely chopped flat-leaf parsley, plus extra to serve
½ green cabbage (450 g), cut into 4 wedges

5 IN 5 PANTRY STAPLES

1 tablespoon extra-virgin olive oil
¼ teaspoon chilli flakes, plus a pinch extra to serve
sea salt and freshly ground black pepper

SERVES 2

THE STATS PER SERVE

Cals: 185
Protein: 3.6 g
Fat: 9.5 g
Carbs: 23.6 g

DF GF PB RSF

Preheat the oven to 220°C and line a baking tray with baking paper.

To make a cabbage marinade, whisk together the olive oil, chilli flakes, garlic, mustard, maple syrup and parsley in a large bowl. Add the cabbage wedges and use your hands to massage the marinade into and between the leaves.

Arrange the cabbage on the tray, keeping some space between each wedge so they crisp up, then pour any remaining marinade on top. Season with salt and pepper and roast for 30 minutes, turning after 15 minutes, or until golden brown around the edges and cooked all the way through. Serve with a sprinkle of extra parsley and eat immediately. Store leftovers in an airtight container in the fridge and enjoy for lunch the next day.

NEXT LEVEL IT: I love adding texture to recipes like this; toasted walnuts or pecans, roughly chopped and sprinkled on top, work an absolute treat.

PRO TIP: Red cabbage works wonderfully in this dish too. Please feel free to mix it up.

This is such a simple yet delicious recipe. The cabbage – which, let's face it, can be pretty dull on its own – is transformed into a hero on the plate.

SWEET POTATO NUGGETS

YOU WILL NEED

2 sweet potatoes (400 g), peeled and cut into 3 cm cubes
2 eggs
1 teaspoon smoked paprika
1 tablespoon desiccated coconut
3 tablespoons sugar-free tomato sauce (see Pro Tip)

5 IN 5 PANTRY STAPLES

3 tablespoons tapioca flour
sea salt and freshly ground black pepper
3 tablespoons almond flour
2 teaspoons extra-virgin olive oil spray

SERVES 2

THE STATS PER SERVE

Cals: 398
Protein: 12.6 g
Fat: 19.6 g
Carbs: 43.4 g

DF GF RSF

Preheat the oven to 180°C and line a baking tray with baking paper.

Cook the sweet potato in a saucepan of boiling water for 6–8 minutes, or until tender. Drain, transfer to a large bowl and allow to cool slightly. Stir in 1 egg, the paprika, half the tapioca flour and a generous pinch of salt and pepper, mix and mash well to make a thick, workable paste. Use your hands to roll heaped tablespoon amounts (about 35 g each) into balls or even-sized nugget shapes. Set aside and get on to setting up your crumbing station.

Whisk the remaining egg in a shallow bowl and, in another shallow bowl, create the crumb by combining the remaining tapioca flour with the almond flour and desiccated coconut.

Dunk each sweet potato nugget into the egg mixture, then coat in the crumb mixture, making sure you get good all-over coverage. Transfer to the tray, spray with the olive oil and bake for 15–20 minutes, turning halfway through, until golden brown, crispy and crunchy on all sides.

Tip the nuggets onto a plate, season with a generous pinch of salt and pepper and serve alongside the tomato sauce.

NEXT LEVEL IT: Try adding extra or different spices – like ground cumin, ground coriander or curry powder – to your nugget mixture for new flavour combinations.

PRO TIP: Sugar-free tomato sauce made with high-quality ingredients and sweetened with monk fruit is a game changer. Make sure you read the labels to get the best stuff.

If you're going to eat sweet potato, it may as well be in nugget form, am I right? Enjoy these – they're on high rotation in my kitchen.

It's no secret that I'm a fan of Mexican flavours, and this nacho bowl celebrates them in a really simple, yet very delectable way.

NEXT-LEVEL NACHO BOWL

YOU WILL NEED

200 g butternut pumpkin, peeled and deseeded
1 tablespoon Mexican seasoning
1 tomato, finely diced
½ small avocado, finely diced
2 tablespoons coriander leaves

5 IN 5 PANTRY STAPLES

2 teaspoons extra-virgin olive oil
1 tablespoon tapioca flour
sea salt and freshly ground black pepper
juice of 1 lemon or lime
pinch of chilli flakes (optional)

SERVES 1

THE STATS PER SERVE

Cals: 392
Protein: 6.5 g
Fat: 25.5 g
Carbs: 42.9 g

DF GF LC RSF

Preheat the oven to 200°C and line a large baking tray with baking paper.

Cut the pumpkin into 3–4 mm thick slices, then cut into irregular triangle shapes and transfer to a large bowl. Add the olive oil and toss to coat well. Now add half the Mexican seasoning, the tapioca flour and a generous sprinkle of salt. Massage with your hands to get even coverage.

Arrange the pumpkin triangles in a single layer on the tray, allowing plenty of space between each slice for maximum crispiness. Bake for 20–30 minutes, or until crispy and golden brown.

Meanwhile, to make a salsa, combine the tomato, avocado, coriander, the remaining Mexican seasoning and the lemon or lime juice in a bowl and gently toss.

Serve the pumpkin chips in a shallow bowl, loaded with the Mexican salsa, sprinkled with the chilli flakes, if using, and seasoned well with salt and pepper.

NEXT LEVEL IT: Looking to increase your healthy fats? Sour cream, yoghurt or cashew cheese are delish additions.

PRO TIP: The thinner you cut the pumpkin, the crispier your chips will be – just keep an eye on them in the oven, as they can burn easily.

SPICY STUFFED MUSHROOMS

YOU WILL NEED

4 large portobello mushrooms, stems removed and reserved
1 garlic clove, crushed
1 long red chilli, finely diced
3 tablespoons raw pistachio kernels
2 tablespoons roughly chopped flat-leaf parsley, plus extra leaves to serve

5 IN 5 PANTRY STAPLES

1 tablespoon extra-virgin olive oil
zest and juice of 1 lemon
sea salt and freshly ground black pepper
¼ teaspoon chilli flakes, to serve (optional)

SERVES 2

THE STATS PER SERVE

Cals: 260
Protein: 10.7 g
Fat: 20 g
Carbs: 10.7 g

DF GF LC PB RSF

Preheat the oven to 200°C and line a large baking tray with baking paper.

Combine the mushroom stems, garlic, chilli, pistachios and 1 tablespoon of the parsley with the olive oil and lemon juice in a high-speed food processer and blitz until a rough, wet paste forms.

Place the mushrooms, gill-side up, on the tray and evenly spoon the paste mixture on top. Season with salt and pepper, then bake for 15–20 minutes, or until the mushrooms are tender and the filling on top has formed a lovely golden crust.

Serve the stuffed mushrooms with a sprinkle of the extra parsley, a pinch of salt and pepper, the lemon zest and the chilli flakes, if using. Store leftovers in an airtight container in the fridge and eat for lunch the next day.

NEXT LEVEL IT: If you enjoy cheese, adding 3 tablespoons of grated parmesan or tasty cheese to the filling mixture really is delicious.

PRO TIP: The pistachios can be subbed out for any other favourite nuts – macadamias or walnuts are great here.

Mushrooms are a really great source of gut-loving bacteria that assist our overall health, and there's no better way to enjoy them than in this super easy recipe.

CAJUN CAULIFLOWER CLUSTERS

YOU WILL NEED

2 teaspoons Cajun spice mix (see Pro Tip)
125 ml (½ cup) sparkling or soda water
½ head of cauliflower (400 g), broken into bite-sized florets
3 tablespoons sugar-free barbecue sauce

5 IN 5 PANTRY STAPLES

120 g (1 cup) tapioca flour
½ teaspoon baking powder
½ teaspoon sea salt
125 ml (½ cup) extra-virgin olive oil

SERVES 2

THE STATS PER SERVE

Cals: 477
Protein: 4.4 g
Fat: 24 g
Carbs: 62.6 g

DF GF LC PB RSF

Combine the tapioca flour, Cajun spice mix, baking powder and salt in a bowl and mix well. Whisk in the sparkling or soda water to make a smooth batter the consistency of pouring cream. Add the cauliflower and mix with your hands to get generous all-over coverage.

Heat the olive oil in a large, deep frying pan over medium–high heat until it reaches 180°C or a small piece of batter sizzles when added. Working in two batches, add the cauliflower clusters and fry, turning often, for 6–8 minutes, or until golden brown and cooked through. Drain on paper towel.

Sprinkle the cauliflower clusters with a generous pinch of salt and serve with the barbecue sauce alongside. Store leftovers in an airtight container in the fridge and enjoy for lunch the next day.

NEXT LEVEL IT: A sprinkle of smoked paprika and some coriander leaves are a lovely addition.

PRO TIP: If your local shop doesn't have a good-quality Cajun spice mix, make your own. Combine 1 tablespoon paprika, 2 teaspoons each of garlic powder and sea salt, 1 teaspoon each of cayenne pepper, onion powder, dried oregano and dried thyme with a generous crack of black pepper. Use what you need for this recipe, then store the rest in a small airtight container for the next time you make this – because you will!

No vegetable has had a bigger glow-up in the last decade than cauliflower. What was once Grandma's boring food is now very trendy, especially in this form.

Getting your greens into your day isn't always fun – well, not as fun as, say, pizza – but this curry may just twist your arm and convince you that they actually are delish.

Serve this curry straight up, or pair with some jasmine rice to up the carbs, or cauliflower rice to keep it low carb and low cal.

GORGEOUS GREEN CURRY

YOU WILL NEED

200 g (2 cups) broccoli florets
1 tablespoon green curry paste (see Pro Tip)
110 g (1 cup) sliced zucchini
40 g (2 cups) roughly chopped English spinach
3 tablespoons coconut cream

5 IN 5 PANTRY STAPLES

2 teaspoons extra-virgin olive oil
125 ml (½ cup) filtered water
sea salt and freshly ground black pepper

SERVES 1

THE STATS PER SERVE

Cals: 442
Protein: 18.5 g
Fat: 29.1 g
Carbs: 42 g

DF GF LC PB RSF

Heat the olive oil in a saucepan over medium–high heat, add the broccoli and cook, stirring occasionally, for 3–4 minutes, or until lightly caramelised on the outside. Add the curry paste and zucchini, stir them in and cook for 4–5 minutes, or until the veggies begin to soften and everything is aromatic.

Add the spinach to the pan, stir and cook for 1 minute, or until lightly wilted, then pour in the coconut cream and water, add a pinch of salt and pepper and reduce the heat to medium. Simmer for 8–10 minutes, or until the sauce has thickened and the vegetables are cooked through.

To serve, spoon the curry into a serving bowl and enjoy.

NEXT LEVEL IT: Got some extra ingredients on hand? Swap the water for chicken bone broth, and add a dash of fish sauce and coconut aminos. Serve with some finely chopped coriander and you're set.

PRO TIP: Not all curry pastes are created equal – look for one with no or minimal vegetable oils and no added sugars.

ULTIMATE GREEN SALAD

YOU WILL NEED

2 baby cos lettuces, leaves separated
90 g (2 cups) mixed salad leaves
1 Lebanese cucumber, sliced into thin wedges
½ avocado, sliced into thin wedges
1 tablespoon pumpkin seeds, toasted and roughly chopped

5 IN 5 PANTRY STAPLES

2 tablespoons extra-virgin olive oil
1 tablespoon apple cider vinegar
juice of 1 lemon or lime (optional)
sea salt and freshly ground black pepper

SERVES 2

THE STATS PER SERVE

Cals: 328
Protein: 5.3 g
Fat: 28.5 g
Carbs: 15.1 g

DF GF LC PB RSF

Combine the olive oil, apple cider vinegar, lemon or lime juice and a pinch of salt and pepper in a large bowl. Lightly whisk, then add the lettuce leaves, mixed salad leaves, cucumber and avocado and gently toss to coat in the dressing.

Top the salad with the pumpkin seeds and serve. Store leftovers in an airtight container in the fridge and enjoy for lunch the next day.

NEXT LEVEL IT: Leftover roughly torn herbs work wonderfully tossed through this salad.

PRO TIP: Looking to make this a more satiating meal or snack? Add a can of sustainable fish, some roughly chopped walnuts or some leftover roast veg.

This green salad is going to be your go-to side to any meal, or try it as a delicious snack to up your daily greens. It really is versatile and it's a great way to freshen up your plate and get a load of beneficial antioxidants.

RIDICULOUS ROAST VEG

YOU WILL NEED

110 g (1 cup) roughly chopped sweet potato
120 g (1 cup) roughly chopped butternut pumpkin
110 g (1 cup) roughly chopped desiree potato
½ garlic bulb, cloves unpeeled, separated and smashed
1 small red onion, cut into chunks

5 IN 5 PANTRY STAPLES

2 tablespoons extra-virgin olive oil
¼ teaspoon chilli flakes
sea salt and freshly ground black pepper
1 teaspoon dried parsley

SERVES 2

THE STATS PER SERVE

Cals: 275
Protein: 2.9 g
Fat: 18.5 g
Carbs: 26.5 g

DF GF PB RSF

Preheat the oven to 200°C and line a large baking tray with baking paper.

Place the chopped vegetables in a large bowl and toss with the olive oil, chilli flakes and ½ teaspoon of salt. Tip onto the tray, keeping some space between the veggies so they get nice and crispy, then roast for 25–30 minutes.

Remove the tray from the oven, add the garlic and onion, give everything a good toss and return to the oven to roast for a further 25–30 minutes, or until everything is golden brown, caramelised and cooked all the way through.

Toss the veg in the dried parsley and serve with a generous sprinkle of salt and pepper. Store leftovers in an airtight container in the fridge and enjoy for lunch the next day.

NEXT LEVEL IT: If you've got some woody herbs like rosemary or thyme hanging around, add them with the garlic and onion for extra flavour.

PRO TIP: This recipe is versatile enough to use a variety of different veg, so mix it up and add what you've got to hand – try cherry tomatoes, cauliflower or broccoli florets or a can of drained chickpeas.

Everyone needs a simple go-to roast vegetable recipe in their repertoire and this is mine – seriously no fuss but ridiculously good every time.

Make sure you chop all your vegetables to a similar size so they cook at the same rate, and keep in mind they'll shrink about 25 per cent during the roasting process. I like to keep the skin on my veg for extra fibre.

Yes, you read that right . . . this is my delicious corn equivalent of meat on the bone, but my version is 100 per cent plant based and done in no time at all.

CRISPY MEXICAN CORN RIBS

YOU WILL NEED

2 corn cobs
1 tablespoon Mexican seasoning
3 tablespoons mayonnaise
1 tablespoon chilli sauce
2 tablespoons finely chopped coriander leaves

5 IN 5 PANTRY STAPLES

1 tablespoon extra-virgin olive oil
juice of 1 lime
¼ teaspoon sea salt

SERVES 2

THE STATS PER SERVE

Cals: 384
Protein: 6.6 g
Fat: 28.2 g
Carbs: 32.5 g

DF GF LC PB RSF

Preheat the oven to 200°C and line a large baking tray with baking paper.

Stand each cob on a chopping board, larger end down, then, carefully slicing from the top with a large chef's knife, cut in half lengthways, then in half again, so you have four 'ribs'. Place the corn ribs on the tray and get on to the marinade.

Combine the olive oil and Mexican seasoning in a small bowl and whisk well. Brush it over the corn ribs to evenly cover, then roast for 25–30 minutes, or until golden brown, curly and crispy.

Meanwhile, to make a spicy chilli mayo, whisk together the mayonnaise and chilli sauce in a small bowl.

Plate up the crispy corn ribs, top with a generous squeeze of lime juice, a sprinkle of coriander and a good season of salt and serve with the spicy chilli mayo alongside. Store leftovers in an airtight container in the fridge and enjoy for lunch the next day.

NEXT LEVEL IT: These ribs also work a treat cooked in an air fryer at 200°C for 15 minutes, turning them halfway through.

PRO TIP: If you can't find a good-quality Mexican seasoning, simply make your own with dried spices, such as chilli powder, ground cumin, ground coriander and smoked paprika.

SALTY CHARRED GREENS

YOU WILL NEED

2 garlic cloves, crushed
6 anchovy fillets
200 g broccolini, trimmed
200 g asparagus, woody ends trimmed
1 tablespoon raw pistachio kernels, roughly chopped

5 IN 5 PANTRY STAPLES

1 tablespoon extra-virgin olive oil
¼ teaspoon chilli flakes
juice of ½ lemon
sea salt and freshly ground black pepper

SERVES 2

THE STATS PER SERVE

Cals: 196
Protein: 10.1 g
Fat: 14.3 g
Carbs: 10.6 g

DF GF LC RSF

Heat the olive oil in a large frying pan over medium–high heat, add the garlic and chilli flakes and cook, stirring occasionally, for 1–2 minutes, or until the garlic starts to turn golden brown. Add the anchovies, use your spoon to break them up and cook for a further 1–2 minutes.

Add the broccolini, asparagus and 2 tablespoons of water to the pan, cover with a lid and reduce the heat to medium. Cook for 6–8 minutes, or until the veggies are cooked through but still have a slight crunch. Remove the lid, add the pistachios and cook for 2–3 minutes, or until the pistachios are lightly toasted and the greens have some char.

Serve the greens with a generous squeeze of lemon juice and a sprinkle of salt and pepper. Store leftovers in an airtight container in the fridge and enjoy for lunch the next day.

NEXT LEVEL IT: Swap out the chilli flakes for chopped fresh chilli to add a lovely depth of flavour.

PRO TIP: This recipe works well with broccoli, cauliflower and even dark leafy greens like kale, silverbeet or English spinach.

I am all for steamed greens on occasion, but charring them adds such a moreish texture and flavour profile – and the anchovies are just salty, heavenly goodness.

FIVE IN FIVE

FIS

SH

SMASHED SALMON SALAD

YOU WILL NEED

200 g baby chat potatoes, skin on
4 eggs
1 baby cos lettuce, leaves separated
100 g hot-smoked salmon fillet, skin removed
2 tablespoons mayonnaise

5 IN 5 PANTRY STAPLES

1 tablespoon extra-virgin olive oil
sea salt and freshly ground black pepper
juice of 1 lemon
¼ teaspoon chilli flakes (optional)

SERVES 2

THE STATS PER SERVE

Cals: 555
Protein: 26.7 g
Fat: 35.3 g
Carbs: 33.8 g

DF GF LC RSF

Preheat the oven to 220°C. Line a baking tray with baking paper.

Cook the potatoes in a large saucepan of salted boiling water for 15–20 minutes, or until they can be easily pierced with a fork. Carefully remove them with tongs, reserving the water to boil your eggs, and pat dry with a clean tea towel.

Transfer the potatoes to the tray, leaving some space between each one. Use a fork or potato masher to smash and flatten them until about 1.25 cm thick – the thinner the smashed potato, the crispier it'll get. Drizzle with the olive oil, season well with salt and pepper and bake for 20–25 minutes, or until golden brown and crispy around the edges.

Bring the water from the potatoes to the boil, add the eggs and cook to your liking – 4 minutes for soft boiled, 6 minutes for medium and 8 minutes for hard boiled. (I like medium for this recipe as the yolk is still oozy.) Set aside to cool.

Layer and overlap the lettuce leaves on one side of a share platter. Place the potatoes alongside the lettuce, then break the salmon into smaller chunks and scatter over the potatoes. Carefully peel and halve your eggs and place them on the potatoes. Top with dollops of mayonnaise, a generous squeeze of lemon juice, a sprinkle of chilli flakes, if using, and a good season of salt and pepper. Use the lettuce leaves as cups to wrap around the potato, salmon and eggs so you can enjoy all the flavours in each bite. Store leftovers in an airtight container in the fridge and eat for lunch or dinner the next day.

NEXT LEVEL IT: Try sprinkling on some chopped dill and chopped toasted nuts.

PRO TIP: Hot-smoked salmon fillets are available at most grocery stores where you find smoked salmon slices. Look for chunky fillets so they look nice and substantial on the plate.

What's not to love here? The crispiest golden chat potatoes you'll ever taste, loaded with delicious smoked salmon and mayo, and all wrapped up in a crisp lettuce cup. Yum!

Here, I'm taking you back to peak paleo days, circa 2013, when zucchini noodles took the world by storm. Using zucchini instead of spaghetti makes this the perfect low-carb and low-cal meal.

SALMON ZAGHETTI

YOU WILL NEED

2 garlic cloves, crushed
400 g can cherry tomatoes (see Pro Tip)
2 small zucchini (250 g), spiralised into thin zoodles
120 g hot-smoked salmon fillet, skin removed, broken into smaller chunks
1 small handful of basil leaves

5 IN 5 PANTRY STAPLES

1 tablespoon extra-virgin olive oil
¼ teaspoon chilli flakes
sea salt and freshly ground black pepper

SERVES 2

THE STATS PER SERVE

Cals: 258
Protein: 13.9 g
Fat: 17.5 g
Carbs: 8.1 g

DF GF LC RSF

Heat the olive oil in a frying pan over medium–high heat, add the garlic and cook, stirring occasionally, for 3–4 minutes, or until caramelised and lightly golden brown. Add the cherry tomatoes and cook, stirring every now and then, for 5–6 minutes, or until bubbling and starting to reduce.

Add the spiralised zucchini, salmon chunks and half the basil to the pan and cook, stirring occasionally, for 4–5 minutes, or until everything is warmed through.

Divide the salmon zaghetti between two plates, top with the remaining basil and add a sprinkle of chilli flakes and a pinch of salt and pepper. Store leftovers in an airtight container in the fridge and enjoy for lunch or dinner the next day.

NEXT LEVEL IT: For a lovely citrus touch, stir in the zest and juice of 1 lemon when you add the salmon.

PRO TIP: You can find canned cherry tomatoes in most supermarkets and grocery stores. They are naturally much sweeter and more flavoursome than crushed tomatoes or passata.

ONE-PAN TUNA PASTA BAKE

YOU WILL NEED

240 g gluten-free mezze maniche rigate (large pasta tubes)
700 g tomato and basil passata
1 tablespoon dried Italian herbs
400 g canned tuna chunks in olive oil, drained
75 g (½ cup) coarsely grated low-fat mozzarella

5 IN 5 PANTRY STAPLES

½ teaspoon chilli flakes
sea salt and freshly ground black pepper
2 teaspoons extra-virgin olive oil

SERVES 4

THE STATS PER SERVE

Cals: 514
Protein: 68 g
Fat: 13.1. g
Carbs: 61.4 g

DF* GF RSF

Preheat the oven to 180°C.

Bring a saucepan of salted water to the boil, add the pasta and cook for 2 minutes less than the packet instructions recommend. Drain and rinse (so the pasta tubes don't stick together), then set side.

Place a large ovenproof frying pan over medium–high heat, add the passata, Italian herbs, chilli flakes and a generous pinch of salt and pepper and stir to combine. Cook for 4–5 minutes, or until the sauce begins to thicken.

Gently stir the pasta and tuna chunks into the sauce and remove the pan from the heat. Drizzle with the olive oil, sprinkle on the cheese and season with a touch more salt. Bake for 15–20 minutes, or until the top is golden brown and the cheese has melted into a crunchy crust. Now dig in! Store leftovers in an airtight container in the fridge and enjoy for lunch or dinner the next day.

NEXT LEVEL IT: To make this extra special, add some basil leaves to the sauce and scatter more over the top to serve.

PRO TIP: For a dairy-free version, swap the cheese for 50 g (½ cup) gluten-free breadcrumbs.

Whenever I think of tuna pasta bake, I think of my amazing mum and some of the incredible one-pan dinners she whipped up for her four hungry sons. I hope I do you proud, Mum.

THAI-STYLE FISH CAKES

YOU WILL NEED

400 g butternut pumpkin, peeled and cut into 2 cm cubes
2 eggs
1 tablespoon red curry paste
250 g canned tuna chunks in olive oil, drained
3 tablespoons aioli or mayonnaise

5 IN 5 PANTRY STAPLES

2 tablespoons extra-virgin olive oil
3 tablespoons tapioca flour
2 tablespoons almond flour
sea salt and freshly ground black pepper

SERVES 4

THE STATS PER SERVE

Cals: 346
Protein: 21 g
Fat: 23.9 g
Carbs: 14.8 g

DF GF LC RSF

Preheat the oven to 200°C and line a baking tray with baking paper.

Place the pumpkin on the tray, coat with half the olive oil and bake for 15–20 minutes, or until soft enough to mash easily with a fork. Set aside to cool slightly.

Combine 1 egg, the curry paste and 1 tablespoon of the tapioca flour in a large bowl and whisk well. Now add the pumpkin and roughly mash with a fork – you don't want a puree, so keep a few bits of pumpkin chunky for texture. Tip in the tuna and, keeping some chunks for texture, stir to form a thick, slightly wet batter.

Roll 80 g (¼ cup) amounts of the batter into eight balls, then flatten slightly and place on a plate. Line up three shallow bowls: add the remaining tapioca flour to one, whisk the remaining egg in another and place the almond flour in the third.

Dunk each fish cake in the tapioca flour, then in the egg and finally, for a lovely golden crust, in the almond flour.

Heat the remaining olive oil in a large frying pan over medium–high heat, add the fish cakes, in batches if needed, and fry on each side for 1–2 minutes to seal and get some colour. Transfer to the tray you used earlier and bake for 10 minutes, or until the fish cakes are cooked through and golden brown.

Season the fish cakes with salt and pepper and serve with the aioli or mayonnaise. Store leftovers in an airtight container in the fridge and enjoy for lunch or dinner the next day.

NEXT LEVEL IT: Finely chopped coriander works wonderfully in the fish cake mixture and coriander sprigs add vibrancy when served alongside.

PRO TIP: I use a store-bought red curry paste that doesn't contain any added sugars or vegetable oils. Read the labels and choose wisely and you will reach your health goals.

Oh, how I *love* good fish cakes, especially when they're as mouth-wateringly crispy and golden as these bad boys. The perfect snack or meal when paired with a vegetable-rich side.

When I was a kid, my family took Friday night fish and chips very seriously. It was a non-negotiable, followed up with a block of Snack chocolate. These days, though, I want to enjoy the same great flavours, but not at the cost of my goals. Fish 'n' fries *and* get results? Yes please.

FISH 'N' FRIES IN A FLASH

YOU WILL NEED

2 sweet potatoes (400 g), peeled and cut into 5 mm matchsticks
1 tablespoon garlic and herb seasoning (see Pro Tip)
1 egg
300 g white fish fillets (whiting, flathead and hoki work well), skin removed and pin-boned
3 tablespoons sugar-free tomato sauce

5 IN 5 PANTRY STAPLES

1 tablespoon extra-virgin olive oil
3 tablespoons tapioca flour
2 tablespoons almond flour
sea salt and freshly ground black pepper
juice of 1 lemon

SERVES 2

THE STATS PER SERVE

Cals: 504
Protein: 37.5 g
Fat: 18.5 g
Carbs: 61.2 g

DF GF RSF

Preheat the oven to 180°C and line a large baking tray with baking paper.

Place the sweet potato in a large bowl and coat with 2 teaspoons of the olive oil. Add 1 tablespoon of the tapioca flour and 2 teaspoons of the garlic and herb seasoning and toss to get good all-over coverage. Arrange the sweet potato on the tray, leaving some space between each piece for ultimate crispness, then bake for 15 minutes.

Now is a good time to set up a crumbing station. Place the remaining tapioca flour in one bowl, whisk the egg in another bowl and combine the almond flour, the remaining garlic and herb seasoning and a pinch of salt in a third bowl.

Working in small batches, roll the fish fillets in the tapioca flour, gently pressing it on for good coverage, then dunk in the egg wash and finally coat with the almond crumb. Place on a plate and set aside.

Once the fries have baked for 15 minutes, remove the tray from the oven. Flip the fries and make some space in the middle. Place the crumbed fish fillets in the gap, spray or drizzle with the remaining olive oil and bake for 15 minutes, turning the fish after about 7 minutes, until the fries are deep golden and the fish has a lovely golden-brown crust and is cooked through.

Serve the fish and fries with the tomato sauce, a squeeze of lemon juice and a generous season of salt and pepper. Store leftovers in an airtight container in the fridge and enjoy for lunch or dinner the next day.

NEXT LEVEL IT: Add colour and freshness to the plate with some baby cos lettuce leaves tossed with a little lemon juice and olive oil.

PRO TIP: I use a really good store-bought garlic and herb seasoning that contains dried garlic, ground coriander, paprika, dried thyme, dried basil, dried parsley, chilli powder and no nasties. Look for something similar or make your own blend.

BANGKOK BARRAMUNDI IN A BAG

YOU WILL NEED

100 g butternut pumpkin, cut into 5 mm thick triangle shapes
1 x 125 g barramundi fillet, skin removed and pin-boned
1 tablespoon red curry paste
100 g canned cherry tomatoes
2 tablespoons finely chopped coriander leaves

5 IN 5 PANTRY STAPLES

2 teaspoons extra-virgin olive oil
sea salt and freshly ground black pepper
juice of 1 lime (optional)

SERVES 1

THE STATS PER SERVE

Cals: 325
Protein: 31.1 g
Fat: 15 g
Carbs: 14.1 g

DF GF LC RSF

Preheat the oven to 200°C and line a baking tray with baking paper.

Place a 40 cm x 30 cm piece of baking paper on your benchtop. To create your base, in the middle of the paper add a layer of the pumpkin triangles roughly the same width and length as the barramundi fillet. Drizzle with 1 teaspoon of the olive oil, then top with the barramundi.

Combine the red curry paste, cherry tomatoes and three-quarters of the coriander in a small bowl and gently whisk. Pour this mixture over the barramundi, drizzle with the remaining olive oil and season well with salt and pepper.

Bring the corners of the baking paper together and twist to enclose, then tie tightly with kitchen twine to seal in the flavours. Place on the tray and bake for 20 minutes. To check, gently open the parcel (be careful of the hot steam) – if the fish is opaque and the pumpkin is tender when pierced with the tip of a knife, it's ready. If not, bake for another 5 minutes and check again.

Allow the barramundi in a bag to rest for 5 minutes, then untie the twine and carefully open – be prepared for the amazing aroma to hit you. Sprinkle with the remaining coriander, add a squeeze of lime juice, if desired, and enjoy.

NEXT LEVEL IT: To up your daily greens, place a handful of roughly chopped baby spinach or kale between the pumpkin and fish – it'll wilt down beautifully during the baking process.

PRO TIP: Barramundi is a great choice as it holds its shape and is fairly robust and firm; salmon and ocean trout work well too.

When I say 'Bangkok', I want you to envision the vibrant, bold and exotic flavours of Thai street food. I've tried to capture a taste of that electricity in this fish parcel.

INDIAN-SPICED OCEAN TROUT

YOU WILL NEED

300 g cauliflower florets (the smaller the better)
1 tablespoon Indian curry powder (see Pro Tip)
2 x 100 g ocean trout fillets, skin removed and pin-boned
1 Lebanese cucumber, sliced into thin ribbons
3 tablespoons plain Greek yoghurt

5 IN 5 PANTRY STAPLES

1 tablespoon extra-virgin olive oil
2 tablespoons tapioca flour
juice of 1 lemon
sea salt and freshly ground black pepper

SERVES 2

THE STATS PER SERVE

Cals: 388
Protein: 28.9 g
Fat: 20.1 g
Carbs: 27.4 g

GF LC RSF

Preheat the oven to 200°C and line a large baking tray with baking paper.

Place the cauliflower in a large bowl and coat well with half the olive oil. Add half the curry powder and 1 tablespoon of the tapioca flour and mix well. Tip the spiced cauliflower onto the tray and spread out to form a single layer.

Add the trout to the same bowl and coat with the remaining olive oil, curry powder and tapioca flour. Place the trout on the tray, leaving some space between each fillet, and bake for 15 minutes, or until the fish is cooked through and has a golden-brown crust. (The flesh should pull apart easily and be opaque in the middle when cooked through – continue cooking for 3–4 minutes if needed.) Transfer the trout to a plate and set aside to rest in a warm place. Increase the oven temperature to 220°C, return the cauliflower to the oven and roast for a further 5–10 minutes, or until golden brown.

Meanwhile, combine the cucumber ribbons, yoghurt and lemon juice in a bowl and gently toss.

Serve the fish and crispy cauliflower with the cucumber salad on the side, seasoned well with salt and pepper. Store leftovers in an airtight container in the fridge and enjoy for lunch or dinner the next day.

NEXT LEVEL IT: Stir roughly torn coriander through the cucumber salad and sprinkle a small handful over the finished dish.

PRO TIP: I use an Indian curry powder I buy from the supermarket that's a combination of ground and dried spices and includes coriander, garlic, turmeric, cumin, onion, paprika, fenugreek, ginger, cinnamon and chilli. Look for something similar or create your own.

This dish is so easy to prepare, but what I love most about it is that everything cooks on the same tray in the oven. It's the type of meal that feels way fancier than the minimal effort required.

Everyone has to have at least one crispy skin fish recipe up their sleeve, and I hope this is the one for you.

The broccoli and pea puree never disappoints and is a vibrant way to get your daily greens.

CRISPY SKIN SALMON WITH BROCCOLI & PEA PUREE

YOU WILL NEED

1 x 100 g salmon fillet, skin on and pin-boned
3 tablespoons chicken bone broth
30 g (½ cup) broccoli florets
70 g (½ cup) frozen peas
45 g (1 cup) mixed salad leaves

5 IN 5 PANTRY STAPLES

2 teaspoons extra-virgin olive oil
sea salt and freshly ground black pepper
juice of 1 lemon (optional)

SERVES 1

THE STATS PER SERVE

Cals: 416
Protein: 28.5 g
Fat: 23.5 g
Carbs: 15.5 g

DF GF LC RSF

Heat 1 teaspoon of the olive oil in a small heavy-based frying pan over medium–high heat and add the salmon, skin-side down. Press down lightly on the salmon with a spatula so all the skin comes into contact with the hot pan and cook for 5–6 minutes, or until the skin is crispy and the flesh is almost half cooked through. Carefully flip the salmon and cook for another 4–5 minutes, or to your liking. (If you're using good-quality salmon, you can serve it quite rare.) Set aside to rest in a warm place.

Meanwhile, for the broccoli and pea puree, pour the chicken bone broth into a saucepan and bring to the boil over medium–high heat. Reduce the heat to low, add the broccoli and peas and simmer for 8–10 minutes, or until the broccoli and peas are tender. Remove from the heat, add a pinch of salt and blitz with a hand-held blender until smooth.

Tip the mixed salad leaves into a bowl and gently toss with the lemon juice, the remaining olive oil and a pinch of salt and pepper.

Serve the salmon on the vivid green puree with your salad alongside.

NEXT LEVEL IT: Add a pinch each of ground cumin, chilli powder and smoked paprika to the broccoli and pea puree.

PRO TIP: Salmon is a fattier cut of fish, so if you're looking for a lower calorie version of this meal, swap the salmon for a white fish like barramundi or whiting.

FIVE IN FIVE

CHIC

KEN

BUTTER CHICKEN BOW

YOU WILL NEED

600 g skinless chicken thigh fillets
2 tablespoons butter chicken spice mix (see Pro Tip)
1 small iceberg lettuce or 4 baby cos lettuces
125 g (½ cup) plain Greek yoghurt or dairy-free alternative
8 yellow cherry tomatoes, diced

5 IN 5 PANTRY STAPLES

2 tablespoons extra-virgin olive oil
sea salt and freshly ground black pepper

SERVES 4

THE STATS PER SERVE

Cals: 388
Protein: 40.5 g
Fat: 21.9 g
Carbs: 6.3 g

DF* GF LC RSF

Start by marinating the chicken. Combine the chicken, butter chicken spice mix, olive oil and ½ teaspoon of salt in a bowl and mix well to coat the chicken in all the oil and spices. Cover and set aside in the fridge for a few minutes while you prepare the remaining ingredients.

Break the lettuce into single leaves, then layer three similar-sized leaves on top of each other to create eight lettuce cup bases.

Preheat a chargrill pan or frying pan over medium–high heat, add the chicken and all the marinade and cook for 4–5 minutes, or until cooked at the edges and beautifully charred. Carefully flip and continue to cook for 3–4 minutes, or until cooked through and charred on both sides.

Transfer the chicken to a chopping board and slice into eight even pieces. Distribute evenly between the lettuce cups, then drizzle with the yoghurt and top with the diced cherry tomato. Season well with salt and pepper and serve. Store leftovers in an airtight container in the fridge and enjoy for lunch or dinner the next day.

NEXT LEVEL IT: Sprinkle some coriander or flat-leaf parsley leaves over the butter chicken bow and, for a touch of spice, add a pinch of chilli flakes. Delish.

PRO TIP: Ready-made butter chicken spice mixes are available at supermarkets these days; read the label and avoid any containing refined sugars. If you can't find one that's suitable, simply combine 2 teaspoons each of ground turmeric, garam masala, ground cumin and chilli powder.

Put away those home-delivery menus, this quick and easy recipe is a healthy fusion of two of my ultimate takeaways. I've taken the lettuce-cup presentation of the Chinese staple san choy bow and paired it with the flavours of that family-friendly Indian favourite, butter chicken.

ONE-TRAY ROAST CHOOK & VEG

YOU WILL NEED

1 x 1 kg chicken
400 g kent pumpkin, cut into 5 cm pieces
400 g coliban or desiree potatoes, cut into 5 cm pieces
120 g frozen peas
100 g kale or English spinach, stems removed, leaves roughly torn

5 IN 5 PANTRY STAPLES

1 lemon, quartered
2 tablespoons extra-virgin olive oil
2 teaspoons dried parsley
sea salt and freshly ground black pepper

SERVES 4

THE STATS PER SERVE

Cals: 539
Protein: 31 g
Fat: 33.9 g
Carbs: 29.8 g

DF GF LC RSF

Preheat the oven to 180°C.

Place the chicken, breast-side up, in the centre of a large non-stick roasting tin. Stuff the lemon quarters into the cavity, then drizzle 1 tablespoon of the olive oil over the chicken, sprinkle with the dried parsley, season well with salt and pepper and use your fingers to massage the oil and seasonings all over the chicken. Roast the chicken for 20 minutes.

Meanwhile, combine the pumpkin and potato with the remaining oil and a generous pinch of salt in a large bowl. Use your hands to mix and get all-over coverage on the veg.

Once the chicken has cooked for 20 minutes, carefully remove the tin from the oven and scatter the pumpkin and potato around the chook. Return to the oven to roast for 30 minutes. Remove from the oven, add the peas and kale or spinach and give the other vegetables a good toss. Roast for 10–15 minutes, or until the chicken is golden brown and the juices run clear when the thigh is pierced with the tip of a knife. Allow the chicken to rest for 10–15 minutes before carving into four equal portions.

Serve the roast chicken surrounded by the deliciously crispy veg, perfect peas and softened greens.

NEXT LEVEL IT: Feel free to mix up the veg and add cubed sweet potato, cauliflower florets, sliced red capsicum and red onion. Also, try adding some rosemary or thyme sprigs for extra depth of flavour.

PRO TIP: Calories in chicken vary based on the different cuts; the thigh is fattier, whereas the breast is lower fat. I have calculated the stats based on a balance of all cuts.

I can't go past a classic roast chook, and this one hits the spot every time. Note that making this recipe creates four meals, so enjoy leftovers for lunches throughout the week or freeze so you have a ready-made dinner on hand for a rainy day.

What I love about my recipe for this iconic duo is the way the flavours in the chicken marinade turn simple pub grub into a tasty, almost gourmet, weeknight meal.

SCHNITTY & SLAW

YOU WILL NEED

1 x 250 g chicken breast fillet, halved lengthways and flattened into 2 equal portions
2 tablespoons coconut aminos
3 tablespoons mayonnaise
200 g coleslaw (see Pro Tip)
45 g (½ cup) desiccated coconut

5 IN 5 PANTRY STAPLES

sea salt and freshly ground black pepper
juice of 1 lemon, plus extra lemon wedges to serve
60 g (½ cup) tapioca flour
60 g (½ cup) almond flour
1 tablespoon extra-virgin olive oil

SERVES 2

THE STATS PER SERVE

Cals: 683
Protein: 44.4 g
Fat: 42.3 g
Carbs: 29.4 g

DF GF LC RSF

Place the chicken portions in a bowl, add the coconut aminos and a pinch of salt and mix well to coat evenly. Cover and marinate in the fridge for 5 minutes or so while you get on with the slaw and the crumb.

For the slaw, combine the lemon juice with half the mayonnaise and the coleslaw in a bowl. Use your hands to mix and coat the coleslaw well, then set aside in the fridge until you are ready to serve.

Combine the desiccated coconut, tapioca flour, almond flour and 1 teaspoon of salt in a large bowl and mix well to make a dry crumb.

Place the chicken in the crumb mixture, turning and firmly pressing it onto each piece to evenly coat all over.

Heat the olive oil in a large frying pan over medium–high heat, add the chicken schnitzels, in two batches, if needed, and fry for 4–5 minutes on each side, or until golden brown and cooked through. Season with salt and pepper.

Serve the chicken with the slaw, the remaining mayo and the lemon wedges alongside. Store leftovers in an airtight container in the fridge and enjoy for lunch or dinner the next day.

NEXT LEVEL IT: Fresh or dried herbs and spices are a wonderful addition to the crumbing mixture. If you've got them on hand, ½ teaspoon paprika and ¼ teaspoon chilli powder add a lovely level of spice.

PRO TIP: Most supermarkets and grocery stores stock pre-made coleslaw mixes, saving you lots of time – and chopping.

TANDOORI CHICKEN & CRISPY CAULI

YOU WILL NEED

250 g (1 cup) plain Greek yoghurt or dairy-free alternative
2 tablespoons tandoori spice mix (see Pro Tip)
2 small chicken thigh fillets (200 g total), skin on
½ head of cauliflower, cut into florets
½ small red onion, finely sliced

5 IN 5 PANTRY STAPLES

juice of 1 lemon
1 tablespoon extra-virgin olive oil
1 tablespoon tapioca flour
sea salt and freshly ground black pepper

SERVES 2

THE STATS PER SERVE

Cals: 419
Protein: 47.7 g
Fat: 14.8 g
Carbs: 25.4 g

DF* GF LC RSF

Preheat the oven to 200°C. Line a baking tray with baking paper.

Combine 125 g (½ cup) of the yoghurt, 1 tablespoon of the tandoori spice mix and half the lemon juice in a large bowl and mix well. Add the chicken and mix with your hands to coat in the seasonings. Cover and place in the fridge for 10–15 minutes.

Place the cauliflower in another large bowl, pour on the olive oil and mix well. Add the tapioca flour, the remaining tandoori spice mix and a pinch of salt and gently toss to coat.

Scatter the cauliflower onto the tray, leaving room for the chicken and allowing space for everything to crisp up nicely. Add the marinated chicken and all the marinade, plus half the red onion. Bake for 25–30 minutes, turning the cauliflower after about 12 minutes, until the chicken is cooked through and the cauliflower is golden brown. If you'd like extra crispy skin on the chicken, place it under a hot oven grill for 1–2 minutes.

To make a lemony yoghurt dressing, combine the remaining lemon juice and yoghurt in a small bowl and whisk well.

Serve the chicken and roasted red onion on a bed of cauliflower, scatter with the remaining red onion and top with a generous dollop of lemony yoghurt. Season well with salt and pepper. Store leftovers in an airtight container in the fridge and enjoy for lunch or dinner the next day.

NEXT LEVEL IT: Try adding finely chopped coriander to your lemony yoghurt and scattering some leaves on top of the chicken to serve.

PRO TIP: To make your own tandoori spice mix, simply combine ½ teaspoon cayenne pepper with 1 teaspoon each of smoked paprika, ground coriander, ground ginger, ground cumin, ground turmeric and salt.

This one-tray wonder is the perfect throw-together weeknight meal for when you've had a busy day. I'm not sure what's easier, the cooking or the cleaning up.

CHICKEN SATAY BURGER

YOU WILL NEED

100 g chicken mince
1 tablespoon crunchy peanut butter
1 tablespoon coconut aminos (see Pro Tip)
1 gluten-free burger bun, split in half and toasted
1 Lebanese cucumber, cut into thin ribbons with a mandoline or vegetable peeler

5 IN 5 PANTRY STAPLES

1 tablespoon tapioca flour
pinch of chilli flakes
½ teaspoon sea salt
2 teaspoons extra-virgin olive oil, plus a dash extra for drizzling
1 tablespoon boiling water

SERVES 1

THE STATS PER SERVE

Cals: 558
Protein: 25.6 g
Fat: 26.7 g
Carbs: 49.2 g

DF GF RSF

Combine the chicken mince, tapioca flour, chilli flakes and salt in a bowl and mix well. Shape into a patty and set aside.

Heat the olive oil in a frying pan over medium–high heat, add the chicken patty and cook for 4–5 minutes on each side, or until golden brown and cooked through. Set aside to rest.

Meanwhile, for the satay sauce, whisk together the peanut butter, coconut aminos and boiling water in a small bowl. For a runnier sauce, simply add a touch more boiling water until you reach your desired consistency.

To plate up, start with the burger bun base, add a layer of half the cucumber ribbons, top with the chicken patty and a generous dollop of satay sauce, add the remaining cucumber ribbons, then chuck the bun lid on and take a bite. Yum!

NEXT LEVEL IT: For a lovely addition, mix some finely chopped coriander into the burger patty, then, when assembling the burger, place a few extra leaves on the patty.

PRO TIP: Coconut aminos is a sticky, salty, sweet coconut-based condiment that makes a perfect replacement for maple syrup, soy sauce or fish sauce. You can find it in health-food stores and online.

We often associate burgers with the classic American combo of beef, cheese, pickles and lettuce; my version celebrates classic South-East Asian flavours with the easiest two-ingredient satay sauce you'll ever make.

If you're looking for a quick, simple and completely satisfying meal, my take on chook pesto pasta has you covered with all the flavours you expect – but it's so much better for you.

CHICKEN PESTO PASTA

YOU WILL NEED

120 g gluten-free spaghetti
200 g chicken breast fillet
1 bunch of basil, leaves picked, small leaves reserved to serve
2 garlic cloves, crushed
2 tablespoons pine nuts

5 IN 5 PANTRY STAPLES

3 tablespoons extra-virgin olive oil
sea salt and freshly ground black pepper
¼ teaspoon chilli flakes

SERVES 2

THE STATS PER SERVE

Cals: 671
Protein: 36.8 g
Fat: 42.4 g
Carbs: 50.1 g

DF GF RSF

Bring a saucepan of salted water to the boil, add the pasta and cook for 2 minutes less than the packet instructions recommend. Drain and set the pasta aside, reserving 125 ml (½ cup) of the pasta water.

Heat 1 tablespoon of the olive oil in a large frying pan over medium heat. Add the chicken, season with salt and pepper and cook for 10–12 minutes, turning after about 5 minutes, until golden brown and cooked through. Transfer the chicken to a plate, reserving the juices in the pan. Cover the chicken with foil and rest in a warm place.

To make the pesto, combine the basil leaves, garlic, pine nuts, chilli flakes and the remaining olive oil in a jug and add a generous pinch of salt and pepper. Blitz with a hand-held blender until well combined and a thick wet paste forms.

Place the same pan with all the delicious reserved juices over medium heat, add the pesto and cook, stirring occasionally, for 3–4 minutes, or until aromatic. Stir in the pasta, add some of the reserved pasta water to loosen up the sauce to your desired consistency and cook for 3–4 minutes, tossing and stirring to coat the pasta with the sauce.

Slice the chicken. Plate up the pasta and serve topped with the chicken, a pinch of salt and pepper and the reserved basil leaves. Store leftovers in an airtight container in the fridge and enjoy for lunch or dinner the next day.

NEXT LEVEL IT: If you're a cheese eater, for extra protein and healthy fats, you can add some grated parmesan to the pesto and sprinkle a little more over the top to serve.

PRO TIP: You'll find store-bought pestos are loaded with inflammatory vegetable oils and fillers, which is why making your own is so much better for you.

ONE-PAN HARISSA CHICKEN

YOU WILL NEED

4 small skinless chicken thigh fillets (400 g total)
400 g butternut pumpkin, chopped into rough chunks
2 tablespoons harissa paste (see Pro Tip)
400 g can cherry tomatoes
125 g (½ cup) plain Greek yoghurt or dairy-free alternative

5 IN 5 PANTRY STAPLES

1 tablespoon extra-virgin olive oil
juice of 1 lemon
sea salt and freshly ground black pepper

SERVES 2

THE STATS PER SERVE

Cals: 587
Protein: 58.3 g
Fat: 26.4 g
Carbs: 26.9 g

DF* GF LC RSF

Preheat the oven to 180°C.

Place an ovenproof frying pan over medium–high heat to heat up. Add the olive oil to the hot pan, then add the chicken and cook for 1–2 minutes on each side until sealed and lightly golden brown. Remove the chicken from the pan and set aside.

Add the pumpkin to the pan and cook, turning often, for 3–4 minutes to get some colour and caramelisation happening. Stir in 1 tablespoon of the harissa and cook for 1–2 minutes. Tip in the cherry tomatoes and stir until everything is well combined. Place the chicken on top, transfer to the oven and bake for 20–25 minutes, or until the sauce has thickened and the pumpkin and chicken are cooked through.

Meanwhile, combine the yoghurt, half the lemon juice and the remaining harissa in a small bowl and whisk well. Cover and set aside in the fridge until ready to serve.

Serve the harissa chicken in the pan or on a plate, topped with dollops of harissa yoghurt, a squeeze of lemon juice and a pinch of salt and pepper. Store leftovers in an airtight container in the fridge and enjoy for lunch or dinner the next day.

NEXT LEVEL IT: Garlic and onion form the basis of so many great recipes. For a flavour boost, add 2 crushed garlic cloves and ¼ sliced red onion to the pan with the pumpkin. A sprinkle of herbs to serve will also bring colour and next-level flavour.

PRO TIP: Harissa paste can be found in supermarkets, delis and Asian grocers. The one I use contains only hot red chillies, garlic, coriander, salt and caraway seeds. Read the labels and always go for real food ingredients.

When it comes to international cuisine, I usually lean into South-East Asian flavours, but lately I've been obsessed with harissa – a north African hot chilli paste – and the depth of flavour it brings to recipes.

SPEEDY CHICKEN SOUVA

YOU WILL NEED

2 small skinless chicken thigh fillets (200 g total), cut into 3 cm cubes
1 tablespoon Greek or Tuscan spice mix (see Pro Tip)
1 Lebanese cucumber (150 g), sliced into thin ribbons
1 large tomato (180 g), diced
3 tablespoons plain Greek yoghurt or dairy-free alternative

5 IN 5 PANTRY STAPLES

1 tablespoon extra-virgin olive oil
3 tablespoons tapioca flour
3 tablespoons almond flour
125 ml (½ cup) filtered water
sea salt and freshly ground black pepper
¼ teaspoon chilli flakes (optional)

SERVES 2

THE STATS PER SERVE

Cals: 446
Protein: 31.5 g
Fat: 24.6 g
Carbs: 23 g

DF* GF RSF

Heat 2 teaspoons of the olive oil in a large frying pan over medium heat, add the chicken and half the spice mix and cook, stirring regularly, for 6–8 minutes, or until the chicken is golden brown and cooked through.

For the pita bread, whisk together the tapioca flour, almond flour, water and the remaining spice mix in a small bowl to make a runny batter. Heat the remaining olive oil in a non-stick frying pan over high heat, pour in half the batter and cook for 4–5 minutes, or until crispy around the edge. Flip and cook for 3–4 minutes, or until golden brown and puffed. Transfer to a plate and repeat with the remaining batter.

To plate up, start with a base of pita bread, load with half the cucumber ribbons and tomato, top with half the charred chicken and finish with some dollops of yoghurt. Season well with salt and pepper and scatter on some chilli flakes, if using. Repeat to make two wraps in total. Store leftovers in an airtight container in the fridge and enjoy for a delicious lunch or dinner the next day.

NEXT LEVEL IT: Finely chopped flat-leaf parsley is a lovely addition: add to the chicken while it's cooking, whisk it through the yoghurt, or sprinkle on top to serve.

PRO TIP: Most supermarkets and grocery stores have a spice section offering a Greek or Tuscan blend of garlic, oregano, rosemary and paprika. If you can't find a suitable combination, try making your own with equal parts garlic powder, dried oregano, dried rosemary and sweet paprika.

Fast food doesn't have to contain processed and refined ingredients or be super high calorie. This recipe proves you can whip up your Friday night takeaway easily at home any night of the week.

FIVE IN FIVE

ME

AT

I hope this recipe is a timely reminder that turkey, especially turkey mince, can be found at most supermarkets and is a wonderful way to add variety to your weekly meals. Naturally sweet and low in fat, it's great for making burgers like this.

MIDDLE EASTERN TURKEY BURGER

YOU WILL NEED

100 g lean turkey mince
2 tablespoons harissa paste
3 tablespoons plain Greek yoghurt or dairy-free alternative
1 gluten-free burger bun, split in half
½ baby cos lettuce

5 IN 5 PANTRY STAPLES

1 teaspoon tapioca flour
sea salt and freshly ground black pepper
1 teaspoon extra-virgin olive oil

SERVES 1

THE STATS PER SERVE

Cals: 443
Protein: 35.7 g
Fat: 14.8 g
Carbs: 35.3 g

DF* GF RSF

Combine the turkey mince, half the harissa paste, the tapioca flour and a pinch of salt in a bowl and mix well. Roll the mixture into a ball, then flatten into a thick patty around the same size as your burger bun.

Heat the olive oil in a frying pan over medium–high heat, add the patty and cook for 5–6 minutes on each side, or until golden brown and cooked through.

Combine the remaining harissa paste with the yoghurt in a bowl and whisk well. Toast the burger bun halves under the oven grill until golden brown and lightly charred on both sides.

To serve, cover the burger bun base with the lettuce, add the patty, then finish with a generous dollop of harissa yoghurt. Top with the burger bun lid and you're ready to dig in.

NEXT LEVEL IT: You can really jazz up this burger by adding any of your favourite trimmings – try tomato and/or beetroot slices and maybe even a slice of haloumi.

PRO TIP: Looking to reduce your carbs? Swap out the bun for iceberg lettuce leaves and you've got yourself a low-carb bun-less burger that tastes just as great.

PHUKET PORK & PINEAPPLE SALAD

YOU WILL NEED

2 tablespoons coconut aminos
1 x 250 g lean pork tenderloin fillet
250 g pineapple, cut into wedges
1 Lebanese cucumber (150 g), sliced into ribbons
1 teaspoon roughly chopped toasted peanuts

5 IN 5 PANTRY STAPLES

2 teaspoons extra-virgin olive oil, plus extra for spraying
¼ teaspoon chilli flakes
sea salt and freshly ground black pepper
juice of 1 lime

SERVES 2

THE STATS PER SERVE

Cals: 400
Protein: 33.6 g
Fat: 18.7 g
Carbs: 22.2 g

DF GF RSF

Combine the coconut aminos, half the olive oil, the chilli flakes and a generous pinch of salt in a large bowl and whisk well. Add the pork and turn to coat well.

Heat a chargrill pan over medium–high heat and lightly spray with the extra olive oil. Add the pork and cook, turning every 3–4 minutes and basting regularly with the marinade, for 12–15 minutes, or until golden brown and just cooked through. (Pork tenderloin is a lean cut of meat, so you don't want to overcook it.) Transfer the pork to a plate, cover with foil and set aside to rest before finely slicing.

Tip any remaining marinade into the pan, add the pineapple wedges and cook over medium–high heat for 4–5 minutes on each side, or until the pineapple has lovely char marks and is caramelised.

For the salad, combine the cucumber with the lime juice and the remaining teaspoon of olive oil in a bowl and mix well.

To serve, create a bed of cucumber on each plate, top with the charred pineapple wedges and sliced pork, sprinkle on the toasted peanuts and season well with salt and pepper. Store leftovers in an airtight container in the fridge and enjoy for lunch or dinner the next day.

NEXT LEVEL IT: To add colour and depth of flavour, toss some aromatic Thai mint and Thai basil leaves through your salad and scatter more over the top to serve. Serve with extra lime wedges too.

PRO TIP: If the sun's shining and you've got a barbecue, this recipe can also be cooked on the grill to add an extra smoky flavour.

Fruit as part of a savoury meal can be controversial, I know, especially when it comes to pineapple on pizza. But the pineapple in this pork salad is a big win for me – that combo of sweet and sour takes me back to takeaways when I was a kid.

SENSATIONAL SATAY SKEWERS

YOU WILL NEED

1 x 200 g lean pork tenderloin fillet
2 tablespoons smooth peanut butter
1 tablespoon coconut aminos
1 handful of finely chopped flat-leaf parsley leaves
100 g (½ cup) jasmine rice

5 IN 5 PANTRY STAPLES

sea salt and freshly ground black pepper
2 teaspoons extra-virgin olive oil
¼ teaspoon chilli flakes
2 tablespoons boiling water

SERVES 2

THE STATS PER SERVE

Cals: 536
Protein: 32.8 g
Fat: 22.1 g
Carbs: 48.5 g

DF GF RSF

You'll need eight metal or bamboo skewers for this recipe.

Heat the oven grill to medium–high and line a large baking tray with baking paper.

Slice the pork lengthways into 5 mm thick strips, then thread onto the skewers and place on the tray. Season with salt and pepper and set aside.

To make the satay sauce, combine the peanut butter, coconut aminos, half the parsley, the olive oil, chilli flakes and boiling water in a large bowl and whisk until smooth.

Brush one-quarter of the satay sauce over the pork, reserving the rest for serving. Place the tray under the grill and cook the skewers for 6–8 minutes, turning after about 3 minutes, until the pork is cooked through and caramelised.

Meanwhile, cook the rice following the packet instructions.

Create a bed of rice on each plate, top with the pork skewers, sprinkle with the remaining parsley and serve with the reserved satay sauce. Store leftovers in an airtight container in the fridge and enjoy for lunch or dinner the next day.

NEXT LEVEL IT: Scatter 1 tablespoon of roughly chopped toasted peanuts over the skewers and serve with a wedge of lime.

PRO TIP: If you prefer lower carbs, simply swap the jasmine rice for cauliflower rice.

Peanut butter gets a serious workout in my house, because it lends itself to both sweet and savoury, and there's no better way to sneak it into your day than with these sensational satay skewers that always hit the spot.

Whenever I'm at a good steak restaurant or bistro, I go for that never-fail dinner of steak frites. There's nothing better than a beautifully cooked piece of beef and the crunch of perfectly golden fries. Now you can enjoy them in your own home, any night of the week.

CLASSIC STEAK FRITES

YOU WILL NEED

1 x 125 g sirloin steak
1 small desiree or coliban potato (100 g), peeled and cut into 5 mm matchsticks
1 teaspoon capers, drained and finely chopped
1 garlic clove, crushed
45 g (1 cup) mixed salad leaves

5 IN 5 PANTRY STAPLES

2 teaspoons extra-virgin olive oil, plus a dash extra
sea salt and freshly ground black pepper
½ teaspoon dried parsley (optional)
pinch of chilli flakes

SERVES 1

THE STATS PER SERVE

Cals: 493
Protein: 34.8 g
Fat: 28.3 g
Carbs: 22 g

DF GF RSF

Take the steak out of the fridge 15–20 minutes before you want to cook it and let it come to room temperature.

Preheat the oven to 200°C and line a large baking tray with baking paper.

Place the potato matchsticks, 1 teaspoon of the olive oil and a generous pinch of salt in a large bowl and toss well. Spread out on the tray and roast for 25–30 minutes, or until the fries are golden brown and cooked through.

Meanwhile, using the same bowl, combine the remaining 1 teaspoon of olive oil with the capers, garlic, dried parsley, if using, chilli flakes and a pinch each of salt and pepper and mix well. Add the steak and coat with all the delicious flavourings.

Heat a heavy-based frying pan over medium–high heat, add the steak and cook, turning every 2–3 minutes, for 10–12 minutes, or until charred and caramelised. Transfer the steak to a plate and set aside to rest in a warm place.

Tip any leftover marinade into the pan and cook for 1–2 minutes, or until reduced and syrupy. Pour the pan-fried marinade goodness over the steak. Place the golden-brown fries and the salad leaves alongside the steak, then drizzle the extra olive oil over the salad leaves. Season with pepper and serve at once.

NEXT LEVEL IT: Add 1 teaspoon of wholegrain mustard to the marinade and serve the finished dish with a dollop on top.

PRO TIP: Sirloin is a fairly lean cut of beef – feel free to use an alternative, such as rib eye or porterhouse, but keep an eye on the macros should you go for a fattier choice.

SPICY SPAG MEATBALLS

YOU WILL NEED

250 g lean beef mince
1 tablespoon dried Italian herbs (see Pro Tip)
1 egg
400 g can cherry tomatoes
160 g gluten-free spaghetti

5 IN 5 PANTRY STAPLES

¼ teaspoon chilli flakes
1 teaspoon dried parsley
sea salt and freshly ground black pepper
1 teaspoon extra-virgin olive oil

SERVES 2

THE STATS PER SERVE

Cals: 553
Protein: 24.1 g
Fat: 13.3 g
Carbs: 71.7 g

DF GF LC RSF

Combine the beef, Italian herbs, egg, chilli flakes, dried parsley and a pinch of salt and pepper in a large bowl and mix well. Roll the mixture into eight to 10 evenly sized balls and set aside on a plate.

Heat the olive oil in a large frying pan over medium–high heat, add the meatballs and fry for 1–2 minutes on all sides, turning them often to brown and seal well. Add the cherry tomatoes and cook for 8–10 minutes, or until the sauce has thickened and the meatballs are cooked through.

Meanwhile, bring a saucepan of salted water to the boil, add the pasta and cook for 1 minute less than the packet instructions recommend. Drain, reserving 125 ml (½ cup) of the cooking water. Add the pasta and the reserved water to the meatballs and cook, stirring, for 1–2 minutes until everything is combined.

Plate up your spag and meatballs and serve with a pinch of salt and pepper. Store leftovers in an airtight container in the fridge and enjoy for lunch or dinner the next day.

NEXT LEVEL IT: Add some finely chopped basil or flat-leaf parsley to the meatball mixture and sprinkle some leaves on top to serve.

PRO TIP: Dried Italian herb blends are sold in supermarkets and grocery stores – just make sure there aren't any added sugars, flours or fillers.

If there's anything I love more than a juicy meatball, it's spaghetti – and this recipe, finished with a mouth-watering red sauce, is the perfect combo of both.

SPICY BEEF TACOS

YOU WILL NEED

200 g lean beef mince
1 tablespoon Mexican seasoning
10 yellow cherry tomatoes, finely diced
½ Lebanese cucumber, finely diced
6 gluten-free soft corn tortillas (26 g per tortilla) (see Pro Tip)

5 IN 5 PANTRY STAPLES

2 teaspoons extra-virgin olive oil
sea salt and freshly ground black pepper
¼ teaspoon chilli flakes
juice of 1 lime

SERVES 2

THE STATS PER SERVE

Cals: 371
Protein: 25.1 g
Fat: 12.7 g
Carbs: 40.5 g

DF GF RSF

Heat 1 teaspoon of the olive oil in a frying pan over medium–high heat, add the mince and cook, stirring with a wooden spoon to break up the lumps, for 4–5 minutes, or until browned. Stir in the Mexican seasoning and a pinch each of salt and chilli flakes. Cook for 2–3 minutes, or until fragrant and the mince is caramelised around the edges. Remove from the heat and set aside.

To make a salsa, combine the tomato, cucumber and lime juice with the remaining olive oil and chilli flakes in a bowl and mix well. Set aside to allow the flavours to develop.

Heat another frying pan over medium–high heat and, working in batches, toast the tortillas for 2–3 minutes on each side, or until golden brown and warmed through. Wrap in a clean tea towel to keep warm.

Serve the warm tortillas loaded with the spicy beef mince and zesty salsa. Store leftovers in an airtight container in the fridge and enjoy for lunch or dinner the next day.

NEXT LEVEL IT: Adding some finely diced avocado to the salsa is a great way to get more vitamins, minerals and healthy fats into your day. Serve with a sprinkle of chopped coriander too.

PRO TIP: Naturally gluten-free and authentic Mexican tortillas are readily available these days – some are white corn, some are blue corn. They are sometimes referred to as street tacos 'cos of their cute size.

Send your tastebuds to the beachside food stalls of Tulum and make it Mexican Monday or Taco Tuesday any day at your house with this no-fail alternative to not-so-healthy street tacos.

This is what I like to call a semi-slow-cooked meal. It's not as fussy or time-consuming as something needing hours on the stove, but the time you do give it is returned tenfold in flavour. Pair with your favourite rice, whether that's plain white or low-carb cauliflower rice.

BRILLIANT BEEF RENDANG

YOU WILL NEED

250 g lean blade steak, cut into 4 cm chunks
1 tablespoon red curry paste
400 g can cherry tomatoes
125 ml (½ cup) beef bone broth
400 g kent pumpkin, peeled and cut into 3 cm cubes

5 IN 5 PANTRY STAPLES

2 teaspoons extra-virgin olive oil
¼ teaspoon chilli flakes

SERVES 2

THE STATS PER SERVE

Cals: 499
Protein: 38 g
Fat: 25.7 g
Carbs: 21.4 g

DF GF LC RSF

Heat the olive oil in a large heavy-based saucepan over medium–high heat, add the beef and cook, stirring and turning, for 5–6 minutes, or until browned. Stir in the curry paste and cook for 2–3 minutes, or until aromatic.

Add the cherry tomatoes, beef bone broth and chilli flakes to the pan and bring to the boil. Reduce the heat to low, place the lid on top and simmer for 45 minutes. Remove the lid, crank the heat up to medium, add the pumpkin and cook for about 15–20 minutes, or until the beef is tender, the pumpkin is soft and the sauce is thick and aromatic.

Serve in large bowls as is. Store leftovers in an airtight container in the fridge and enjoy for lunch or dinner the next day.

NEXT LEVEL IT: This dish lends itself to adding heaps of vegetables: diced zucchini and broccoli and cauliflower florets work well – simply add them with the pumpkin. Some toasted shredded coconut and coriander leaves sprinkled over the top are great too.

PRO TIP: This is a great recipe to make in larger quantities and freeze in individual portions, so you have future meals on hand to heat and eat when you need something quick and easy.

LUKEY'S LAMB PIZZA

YOU WILL NEED

1 small red onion (125 g), finely sliced
200 g lean lamb mince
2 tablespoons harissa paste
1 x gluten-free sourdough pizza base
3 tablespoons plain Greek yoghurt or dairy-free alternative

5 IN 5 PANTRY STAPLES

2 teaspoons extra-virgin olive oil
sea salt and freshly ground black pepper
¼ teaspoon chilli flakes

SERVES 2

THE STATS PER SERVE

Cals: 609
Protein: 27.6 g
Fat: 24.3 g
Carbs: 64.1 g

DF* GF RSF

Preheat the oven to 220°C and line a large baking tray with baking paper.

Heat 1 teaspoon of the olive oil in a frying pan over medium–high heat, add half the onion and cook, stirring with a wooden spoon, for 2–3 minutes, or until the onion is softened and caramelised. Add the lamb mince and cook, stirring to break up the lumps, for about 4–5 minutes, or until browned. Stir in 1 tablespoon of the harissa paste, season with salt and pepper and cook for a further 2–3 minutes, or until fragrant.

Now is a good time to par-bake your pizza base. Place it on the baking tray and bake for 5–6 minutes to heat through. This helps make the pizza extra crispy once you add the toppings.

Cover the pizza base with the lamb mixture and bake for 6–8 minutes, or until the base is golden on the edges and the lamb on top is charred.

Whisk the yoghurt and the remaining harissa paste in a small bowl and dollop this randomly over the top of the pizza. Scatter on the remaining onion, sprinkle with the chilli flakes, season with salt and pepper and serve. Store leftovers in an airtight container in the fridge and enjoy for lunch or dinner the next day.

NEXT LEVEL IT: For a splash of colour and added freshness that cuts through the richness of the lamb, scatter flat-leaf parsley or mint leaves on top.

PRO TIP: I use a delicious gluten-free sourdough pizza base that can be found in health-food stores and online. Always read the label of the one you use to make sure you stay on track.

I love a great pizza, and I love using lamb mince as, after it hits the oven, you get this beautiful sticky caramelisation that melts in your mouth with every bite. This is the only pizza you'll need on speed dial.

FIVE IN FIVE

TRE

ATS

ONE-BOWL BANANA BREAD

YOU WILL NEED

3 very ripe bananas (the riper the better)
4 eggs
275 g (2 ½ cups) oat flour
160 g (1 cup) granulated coconut sugar
3 tablespoons walnuts, toasted and roughly chopped

5 IN 5 PANTRY STAPLES

185 ml (¾ cup) extra-virgin olive oil
2 teaspoons baking powder
½ teaspoon salt

SERVES 12

THE STATS PER SERVE

Cals: 347
Protein: 5.5 g
Fat: 19.9 g
Carbs: 35.9 g

DF RSF

Preheat the oven to 180°C and line a 21 cm x 11 cm loaf tin with baking paper.

Place two of the bananas in a large bowl and mash with a whisk until lovely and smooth. Add the eggs and olive oil and whisk until well incorporated. Now add all the dry ingredients, reserving 3 tablespoons of the coconut sugar, and the walnuts, keeping aside a small handful, and mix well with a spoon or spatula to form a thick batter.

Pour the batter into the tin. Slice the remaining banana in half lengthways and place it on top of your loaf, then scatter on the reserved walnuts and coconut sugar (the sugar creates an incredible caramelised top). Bake for 1 hour, or until golden brown on top and a toothpick inserted in the centre comes out clean. Allow to cool slightly before removing from the tin.

Enjoy warm or store in an airtight container in the fridge for up to 5 days or freeze for up to 3 months.

NEXT LEVEL IT: To elevate the flavour of this beautiful loaf, add 1 teaspoon each of vanilla bean paste and ground cinnamon with the dry ingredients.

PRO TIP: Don't have a loaf tin? Simply pour the batter into a standard 12-hole muffin tin lined with paper cases and bake for 18–20 minutes, or until a toothpick inserted in the centre of a muffin comes out clean.

I am obsessed with treat and dessert recipes – like this banana bread – that involve using only one bowl, as they mean less time cleaning up the kitchen and more time eating all that delicious goodness.

Like Batman and Robin, this dynamic duo of chocolate and peanut butter comes together in these no-fuss cookies. And when it comes to something quick and yum, these really pack a punch – BAM, POW, KAPOW!

CHOC PEANUT BUTTER COOKIES

YOU WILL NEED

1 large ripe banana (120 g)
250 g (1 cup) smooth peanut butter
125 ml (½ cup) maple syrup
270 g (3 cups) gluten-free rolled oats (see page 30)
180 g (1 cup) dark chocolate chips

MAKES ABOUT 20

THE STATS PER SERVE (1 cookie = 1 serve)

Cals: 200
Protein: 6.1 g
Fat: 10.7 g
Carbs: 18.4 g

DF GF* PB RSF

Preheat the oven to 180°C and line a large baking tray with baking paper.

Place the banana in a large bowl and mash with a whisk until smooth. Whisk in the peanut butter and maple syrup until well incorporated. Add the oats and almost all the chocolate chips, reserving a few for sprinkling on top, and stir with a wooden spoon or silicone spatula until a thick wet dough forms.

Roll heaped tablespoon amounts of the dough into balls and place on the tray, leaving space between each one for spreading. Lightly press down on each ball to flatten slightly and sprinkle on the reserved chocolate chips. Bake for 12–15 minutes, or until the cookies are golden brown on top and crunchy around the edges. Allow them to cool slightly on the tray, then enjoy. Store in an airtight container in the fridge for up to 5 days or freeze for up to 3 months.

NEXT LEVEL IT: This recipe is the perfect base for delicious additions, such as roughly chopped nuts, shredded coconut or dried fruit.

PRO TIP: In the front of the book, I have some helpful information on navigating rolled oats and if they're actually gluten free – check it out on page 30.

LUKEY'S TARTE TATIN

YOU WILL NEED

125 ml (½ cup) maple syrup
3 tablespoons canned coconut milk
3 tablespoons unsweetened apple juice
1 teaspoon vanilla bean paste
3 granny smith apples (300 g), cored, peeled and quartered

5 IN 5 PANTRY STAPLES

120 g (1 cup) almond flour
3 tablespoons tapioca flour
1 teaspoon baking powder
½ teaspoon sea salt

SERVES 6

THE STATS PER SERVE

Cals: 268
Protein: 4.6 g
Fat: 11.6 g
Carbs: 36.7 g

DF GF RSF

Preheat the oven to 200°C.

For the crust, combine the almond flour, tapioca flour, baking powder, salt and 3 tablespoons of the maple syrup in a bowl. Mix well, adding a little extra maple syrup if needed to bring everything together, until a slightly sticky dough forms. Roll the dough into a ball, place on a piece of baking paper and flatten out with the palm of your hand until it is the same diameter as the ovenproof non-stick frying pan you're using. Set aside.

Place the frying pan over medium heat and add the remaining maple syrup, the coconut milk, apple juice and vanilla, then bring to a simmer and cook for 4–5 minutes. Add the apple and cook, stirring occasionally, for 10–15 minutes, or until the apple begins to soften and the sauce is lovely and sticky.

Remove the pan from the heat. Pick up the baking paper and very carefully flip the crust onto the cooked apple (so the paper is uppermost) and gently press down. Remove the paper and bake for 15–20 minutes, or until the crust is golden brown. Allow the tart to cool slightly. Cover the pan with a large plate, then carefully flip the tart onto the plate so the crust is on the bottom and the sticky and gooey apple goodness is on top. Serve warm and enjoy immediately. I doubt there will be any leftovers, but if there are, store in an airtight container in the fridge for up to 5 days.

NEXT LEVEL IT: A scoop of ice cream or a dollop of vanilla yoghurt or double cream are lovely additions.

PRO TIP: This recipe highlights why having at least one high-quality ovenproof non-stick frying pan can be incredibly useful in your kitchen.

For this recipe, you'll need an ovenproof non-stick frying pan about 20 cm in diameter. Keep in mind that if you use a bigger pan, you'll need to increase your quantities.

NO-BAKE BANOFFEE SLICE

YOU WILL NEED

200 g (1½ cups) raw cashews
300 g (1½ cups) medjool dates, pitted, soaked in boiling water for 15 minutes and drained
2 bananas, sliced diagonally
200 g plain Greek yoghurt, to serve
50 g dark chocolate (85% cacao), shaved

5 IN 5 PANTRY STAPLES

100 g (1 cup) almond flour
2 teaspoons sea salt
3 tablespoons coconut oil

MAKES 12

THE STATS PER SERVE

Cals: 317
Protein: 7.5 g
Fat: 19.7 g
Carbs: 26.3 g

GF RSF

Place the cashews, almond flour and 1 teaspoon of salt in a food processor and blitz to form a coarse flour consistency. Add 100 g (½ cup) of the dates and blitz again until a sticky dough forms.

Line a 22 cm square cake tin with baking paper, then press the dough into the tin so it smoothly and evenly covers the base. Transfer to the freezer to firm up the slice base while you get on to the toffee filling.

For the toffee filling, combine the remaining dates with the coconut oil and 1 teaspoon of salt in the food processor and blitz to make a thick smooth paste. If it's too thick, add a little more coconut oil or water to loosen it. Spoon the toffee filling over the slice base and return to the freezer to set.

To assemble, arrange the sliced banana in a thick layer over the set toffee, then use a hot knife to carefully cut into 12 even slices. Top each slice with a heaped tablespoon of yoghurt, sprinkle with the shaved dark chocolate and enjoy. For best storage instructions, see Pro Tip.

NEXT LEVEL IT: To stop your banana slices browning, place them in a bowl, squeeze on the juice of a lemon and gently mix to coat well. Drain and pat dry, before layering on the toffee.

PRO TIP: If you don't intend to eat this slice within a few days, I recommend you make it as far as the sliced banana, then freeze those leftovers as is, prior to adding any yoghurt or chocolate. When ready to enjoy another piece, remove a slice from the freezer and allow it to soften slightly at room temperature, then top with the yoghurt and chocolate.

I know 'banoffee' is a weird-sounding word, but let me explain – it's a combo of the words 'banana' and 'toffee'. Sounds irresistible, doesn't it? Here, my healthier version of toffee is made from sticky dates. Yummy!

When I hear the words 'black forest' I instantly envision that perfect combo of rich chocolate with succulent cherries. This interpretation takes the traditional cake and turns it into a super easy brownie. You'll love this.

BLACK FOREST BROWNIES

YOU WILL NEED

225 g butter, melted
320 g (2 cups) granulated coconut sugar
4 eggs
120 g (1 cup) cacao powder
140 g (1 cup) frozen pitted cherries

5 IN 5 PANTRY STAPLES

60 g (½ cup) almond flour
60 g (½ cup) tapioca flour
½ teaspoon sea salt

MAKES 16

THE STATS PER SERVE

Cals: 263
Protein: 4.7 g
Fat: 15.3 g
Carbs: 25.5 g

GF RSF

Preheat the oven to 180°C and line a 20 cm square cake tin with baking paper.

Place the melted butter and coconut sugar in a large bowl and whisk until well combined and a lovely caramel colour. Whisk in the eggs until incorporated. Add the cacao powder, almond flour, tapioca flour and salt and mix well with a wooden spoon or silicone spatula until a thick batter forms.

Pour into the tin, then scatter the cherries on top. Bake for 25–30 minutes, or until the top is a little crunchy and the middle is still gooey. Allow to cool in the tin a little before slicing evenly into 16 squares. Enjoy warm, or as snacks on the go. Store in an airtight container in the fridge for up to 5 days or freeze for up to 3 months.

NEXT LEVEL IT: Frozen mixed berries are a great substitute for the cherries – in fact, any fresh or frozen berry combo works well in this recipe.

PRO TIP: For perfectly portioned snacks to eat on the go, replace the cake tin with a standard 12-hole muffin tin and cut the baking time to 10–12 minutes. The muffins are ready when a toothpick inserted in the centre of one comes out with moist crumbs attached.

SPEEDY SELF-SAUCING PUDDINGS

YOU WILL NEED

1 egg
3 tablespoons almond or coconut milk
3 tablespoons granulated coconut sugar
3 tablespoons cacao powder
3 tablespoons roughly chopped dark chocolate (85% cacao)

5 IN 5 PANTRY STAPLES

coconut oil, for greasing
1 tablespoon tapioca flour
1 teaspoon baking powder
pinch of sea salt

SERVES 2

THE STATS PER SERVE

Cals: 372
Protein: 9.8 g
Fat: 18.8 g
Carbs: 36.6 g

DF GF RSF

Preheat the oven to 180°C and grease two 125 ml (½ cup) ovenproof ceramic mugs with coconut oil.

Place the egg, almond or coconut milk, coconut sugar, cacao powder, tapioca flour, baking powder and salt in a bowl and whisk well until wet, gooey and well combined. Pour the batter into the mugs, then press the chocolate into the centre.

Bake the puddings for 5–6 minutes, or until the tops are crunchy and the middle is still moist and gooey. Enjoy immediately. Cover the second pudding and store in the fridge to enjoy the next day.

NEXT LEVEL IT: Want to increase the protein for a post-workout treat? Swap the tapioca flour for a scoop of vanilla or chocolate protein powder.

PRO TIP: If you don't have ovenproof mugs, you can use ceramic ramekins.

You know those nights when you're binge-watching your fave show and you feel like a sweet treat without all the fuss? Well, this is *the* recipe you need for those moments.

BANGIN' BOUNTY-LICIOUS BARS

YOU WILL NEED

270 g (3 cups) fine desiccated coconut
125 ml (½ cup) melted coconut oil
125 ml (½ cup) maple syrup
1 teaspoon vanilla bean paste
150 g dark chocolate (85% cacao)

MAKES 14

THE STATS PER SERVE (1 bar = 1 serve)

Cals: 290
Protein: 1.4 g
Fat: 25.8 g
Carbs: 11.6 g

DF GF PB RSF

For your bounty-licious filling, place the coconut, coconut oil, maple syrup and vanilla in a food processor and pulse until the mixture holds together and is a sticky workable texture. Shape the filling mixture into 14 individual bars, then transfer to a tray lined with baking paper. Place in the freezer for 1 hour, or until set firm.

Break the chocolate into chunks and place in a heatproof bowl set over a saucepan of barely simmering water. Using a silicone spatula, stir until the chocolate is just melted. Remove the bowl from the heat and set aside to cool a little.

Once your bars have set and the chocolate is cool enough to work with, dunk each bar completely in the chocolate, return to the tray and place in the fridge for 15 minutes, or until the chocolate is set. If you've got any leftover chocolate, you can do a second dunk, or drizzle some on top to make cool patterns. Store the bars in an airtight container in the fridge for up to 5 days or freeze for up to 3 months.

NEXT LEVEL IT: These can be transformed into cherry ripe bars by simply thawing and adding 140 g (1 cup) frozen pitted cherries to the filling mixture in the food processor.

PRO TIP: Because these bars are so calorie dense, a little goes a long way – so just a small amount will have you feeling fuller for longer.

I love a Bounty bar, but the classic recipe doesn't fit my macros. So, I've reworked this fan favourite into a nutrient-dense treat that doesn't skimp on flavour.

Every time I make a carrot cake for friends and family they go nuts, so I wanted to share a simplified version in muffin form that I think is . . . tops. Get it? Haha.

CARROT CAKE MUFFINS

YOU WILL NEED

4 eggs
125 ml (½ cup) maple syrup
1 heaped teaspoon ground cinnamon
280 g (2 cups) finely grated carrot
50 g (½ cup) pecans, roughly chopped

5 IN 5 PANTRY STAPLES

3 tablespoons melted coconut oil
240 g (2 cups) almond flour
120 g (1 cup) tapioca flour
1 teaspoon baking powder

MAKES 12 SMALL OR 6 LARGE

THE STATS PER SERVE
(Based on 12 small muffins)

Cals: 291
Protein: 6.7 g
Fat: 19.6 g
Carbs: 21.4 g

DF GF RSF

Preheat the oven to 180°C and line a large six- or standard 12-hole muffin tin with paper cases.

Place the eggs, maple syrup and coconut oil in a large bowl and whisk until light, fluffy and well combined. Add the almond flour, tapioca flour, baking powder and cinnamon and use a wooden spoon or silicone spatula to mix until well incorporated. Fold in the carrot, then spoon the batter evenly into the tin and sprinkle the pecans on top. Bake for 15 minutes for the 12-hole tin or 20 minutes for the 6-hole tin, or until golden brown on top and a toothpick inserted in the centre of a muffin comes out clean.

Allow the muffins to cool slightly before removing from the tin. Store in an airtight container in the fridge for up to 5 days or freeze for up to 3 months.

NEXT LEVEL IT: For extra depth of flavour, add ½ teaspoon each of ground nutmeg, allspice and ground ginger along with the cinnamon.

PRO TIP: If you're looking to increase your nutrients, sprinkling these with toasted shredded coconut gives you extra good fats, and serving them with a generous dollop of high-protein yoghurt is a great addition to your daily energy needs.

THE ULTIMATE APPLE SLICE

YOU WILL NEED

1 very ripe banana
1 egg
160 g (1 cup) granulated coconut sugar
1 teaspoon ground cinnamon
3 granny smith apples (300 g), cored, peeled, and cut into 2 cm cubes

5 IN 5 PANTRY STAPLES

1 tablespoon melted coconut oil
120 g (1 cup) almond flour
60 g (½ cup) tapioca flour
1 teaspoon baking powder

MAKES 8

THE STATS PER SERVE (1 slice = 1 serve)

Cals: 264
Protein: 4.4 g
Fat: 10.1 g
Carbs: 39.3 g

DF GF RSF

Preheat the oven to 180°C and line a 20 cm square cake tin with baking paper.

For the base, place the banana in a large bowl and mash with a whisk until completely smooth. Add the egg and 1 tablespoon of the coconut oil and whisk until incorporated. Add half the coconut sugar, the almond flour, tapioca flour and baking powder and mix with a wooden spoon or silicone spatula until well combined.

Pour the base mixture into the tin, then smooth and flatten the surface so it's nice and even.

Wipe out the bowl, add the remaining coconut sugar, the cinnamon and apple and mix to combine. Tip onto the base, spread out and smooth with a spoon, then bake for 30–40 minutes, or until golden brown and caramelised on top. Slice into eight portions and enjoy. Store in an airtight container in the fridge for up to 5 days or freeze for up to 3 months.

NEXT LEVEL IT: This recipe pairs beautifully with a dollop of vanilla yoghurt or ice cream.

PRO TIP: If you're looking to increase your daily energy intake, add a crumble layer by sprinkling some shredded coconut or roughly chopped nuts over the apple before you pop the slice in the oven.

When I was growing up, there was a bakery near my house that made the *best* apple slice. And now, 30-odd years later, I have recreated it just for you. I hope I do it justice.

ONE-PAN MUD CAKE

YOU WILL NEED

4 eggs
160 g (1 cup) granulated coconut sugar
120 g (1 cup) cacao powder
90 g (½ cup) chopped dark chocolate (85% cacao), melted
4 scoops vanilla ice cream (100 g)

5 IN 5 PANTRY STAPLES

125 ml (½ cup) melted coconut oil, plus extra for greasing
1 teaspoon baking powder
¼ teaspoon sea salt
120 g (1 cup) almond flour

SERVES 10

THE STATS PER SERVE

Cals: 356
Protein: 9.1 g
Fat: 24.8 g
Carbs: 22 g

DF GF RSF

Preheat the oven to 180°C and lightly grease a 20 cm ovenproof non-stick frying pan with coconut oil.

Place the eggs in a large bowl and whisk until light and fluffy. Add the coconut sugar, coconut oil, baking powder and salt and whisk until well combined. Now add the cacao powder and almond flour and mix with a wooden spoon or silicone spatula until incorporated. Bake for 15–20 minutes, or until the top of the cake is crunchy and firm and a skewer inserted in the centre comes out clean.

Set the cake aside to cool slightly. Top with a generous drizzle of melted chocolate and the ice cream. If you've got any leftover chocolate, feel free to drizzle it over the ice cream.

Serve the cake in the pan in the centre of the table with spoons to dig in and share. Leftovers are rare at my house, but if you get too full, store in an airtight container in the fridge for up to 5 days.

NEXT LEVEL IT: You know I'm a massive fan of pairing chocolate with berries. I highly recommend serving this cake topped with fresh berries.

PRO TIP: Larger serve desserts are a timely reminder that we don't need to eat the entire thing. Always take note of my recommended serving size so you don't blow your daily calories.

You know those supermarket mud cakes people go crazy over? Well, now you can create your own healthy version at home. Just keep in mind you'll need an ovenproof non-stick frying pan for this recipe. This is the perfect treat for sharing when you're feeding a crowd.

CONVERSION CHARTS

Measuring cups and spoons may vary slightly from one country to another, but the difference is generally not enough to affect a recipe. All cup and spoon measures are level.

One Australian metric measuring cup holds 250 ml (8 fl oz), one Australian metric tablespoon holds 20 ml (4 teaspoons) and one Australian metric teaspoon holds 5 ml. North America, New Zealand and the UK use a 15 ml (3-teaspoon) tablespoon.

LENGTH

METRIC	IMPERIAL
3 mm	⅛ inch
6 mm	¼ inch
1 cm	½ inch
2.5 cm	1 inch
5 cm	2 inches
18 cm	7 inches
20 cm	8 inches
23 cm	9 inches
25 cm	10 inches
30 cm	12 inches

LIQUID MEASURES

ONE AMERICAN PINT	ONE IMPERIAL PINT
500 ml (16 fl oz)	600 ml (20 fl oz)

CUP	METRIC	IMPERIAL
⅛ cup	30 ml	1 fl oz
¼ cup	60 ml	2 fl oz
⅓ cup	80 ml	2½ fl oz
½ cup	125 ml	4 fl oz
⅔ cup	160 ml	5 fl oz
¾ cup	180 ml	6 fl oz
1 cup	250 ml	8 fl oz
2 cups	500 ml	16 fl oz
2¼ cups	560 ml	20 fl oz
4 cups	1 litre	32 fl oz

DRY MEASURES

The most accurate way to measure dry ingredients is to weigh them. However, if using a cup, add the ingredient loosely to the cup and level with a knife; don't compact the ingredient unless the recipe requests 'firmly packed'.

METRIC	IMPERIAL
15 g	½ oz
30 g	1 oz
60 g	2 oz
125 g	4 oz (¼ lb)
185 g	6 oz
250 g	8 oz (½ lb)
375 g	12 oz (¾ lb)
500 g	16 oz (1 lb)
1 kg	32 oz (2 lb)

OVEN TEMPERATURES

CELSIUS	FAHRENHEIT
100°C	200°F
120°C	250°F
150°C	300°F
160°C	325°F
180°C	350°F
200°C	400°F
220°C	425°F

CELSIUS	GAS MARK
110°C	¼
130°C	½
140°C	1
150°C	2
170°C	3
180°C	4
190°C	5
200°C	6
220°C	7
230°C	8
240°C	9
250°C	10

THANKS

You can't judge a book by its cover, especially when it comes to how much work goes into making it. So although it's my name in bold type on the front – and these are my tried and tested recipes – so much more, and many more people, have made it possible, and it is so important that I thank them.

First off, to you, the readers/home cooks/inspired humans looking for positive change. Simply by picking up this book, and the ones that came before, you've enabled me to follow my passion and made my dreams come true. Because my commitment to inspiring others only goes so far – it takes you guys getting behind me to make it possible on such a scale, and for that I am eternally grateful. Your support never goes unnoticed or unappreciated, and I hope the inspiration, education and delectation I provide in return helps fill your cup.

Now to the dream team, my publishing family, the beautiful humans who bundle up all my ideas/creations/excitement into the book you're holding right now. To my publisher, Mary, thank you for continuing to believe in me and what I am about, and for sharing my obsession with 80s and 90s Australian television personalities and TV's night of nights (both of them). To Clare, my senior editor, my ride or die each step of the way when writing this book, thank you for your guidance, enthusiasm and pure positivity in putting the pieces of the puzzle together – I just love working with you. And to everyone else at Plum – Jane, Charlotte, Allie, the greater sales, marketing and publishing team – thank you, it takes an army.

Shoot week is when all the planning, testing, writing and preparation gets put into practise, with the team of all teams at the helm. We take over an entire studio, and in the kitchen I am joined by the irreplaceable Sarah and Caroline. Thanks to you both for getting my style of food, and for giving it your kiss of experience and expertise. Once the food is cooked, the keen eye for this queer guy is Lee, our food stylist. The biggest thanks to you, Lee, for taking my vision and giving it your unique and special touch of love to elevate it beyond measure. And once it's looking the absolute goods, it's time for our photographer to capture it (and me) in a way that only he can. Marky Mark, this is our eighth book together, and I can't imagine doing any of them without you. You're an absolute legend, professionally and personally.

Along the entire way, Megan, my editor, is there to keep the book in check, from simple things like spelling and grammar, to the big things like making sure my overall message is conveyed in the most clear, accessible and enjoyable way. Megan, you're an absolute star. And to Kirby, my designer, who wraps the entire thing up in a bow with her cover design, internal graphics, fonts and overall vibrance. Kirby, you've done it again. You really are just so good, thank you.

And, of course, to my beautiful circle of loved ones, those of you who have been there through all my ups, downs and everything in between. It is your unconditional love that provides me with the support to be who I am today. Thank you.

INDEX

Pan Macmillan acknowledges the Traditional Custodians of Country throughout Australia and their connections to lands, waters and communities. We pay our respect to Elders past and present and extend that respect to all Aboriginal and Torres Strait Islander peoples today. We honour more than sixty thousand years of storytelling, art and culture.

A Plum book

First published in 2023 by
Pan Macmillan Australia Pty Limited
Level 25, 1 Market Street,
Sydney, NSW 2000, Australia

Level 3, 112 Wellington Parade,
East Melbourne, VIC 3002, Australia

Designed and typeset by Kirby Armstrong
Edited by Megan Johnston
Index by Helena Holmgren
Photography by Mark Roper
Food and prop styling by Lee Blaylock
Food preparation by Caroline Griffiths, Luke Hines and Sarah Watson
Colour reproduction by Splitting Image Colour Studio
Printed and bound in China by Imago Printing International Limited

A CIP catalogue record for this book is available from the National Library of Australia.

10 9 8 7 6 5 4 3 2 1